The Best of
Black Mountai

Teri Christopherson

Martingale™
& COMPANY

Dedication

For Barbara Brandeburg, my sister, partner, and friend. Barbara has her own quilt pattern company, Cabbage Rose, and we have traveled this wonderful road together. Her friendship, support, and advice mean everything to me.

Acknowledgments

Special thanks to Vicki Stratton, who has beautifully quilted most of the quilts in this book. On numerous occasions she has cheerfully set aside her own interests to help me meet my print deadlines.

Special thanks to Dan Snipes, who has been photographing my quilts from the beginning. He makes my quilts look better than they really are. He is talented, skilled, and fun to work with. (And willing to eat leftover photo props for lunch.)

Mission Statement

We are dedicated to providing quality products and service by working together to inspire creativity and to enrich the lives we touch.

Credits

President	Nancy J. Martin
CEO	Daniel J. Martin
Publisher	Jane Hamada
Editorial Director	Mary V. Green
Managing Editor	Tina Cook
Technical Editor	Kathy Conover
Editorial Assistant	Laurie Bevan
Copy Editor	Allison A. Merrill
Design Director	Stan Green
Illustrator	Laurel Strand
Cover and Text Designer	Regina Girard
Photographers	Dan Snipes
	Brent Kane
Quilting	Vicki Stratton

That Patchwork Place® is an imprint of Martingale & Company™.

The Best of Black Mountain Quilts
© 2002 by Teri Christopherson

Martingale & Company
20205 144th Avenue NE
Woodinville, WA 98072-8478 USA
www.martingale-pub.com

Printed in China
07 06 05 04 03 02   8 7 6 5 4 3 2 1

Library of Congress Cataloging-in-Publication Data
Christopherson, Teri
    The best of Black Mountain quilts / Teri Christopherson.
        p. cm.
    ISBN 1-56477-463-5
1. Patchwork—Patterns. 2. Quilting—Patterns. 3. Appliqué—Patterns. I. Title.
    TT835 .C85 2002
    746.46'041—dc21
                                                                    2002007826

Contents

Introduction

I have been designing quilts and sharing my patterns with quilters around the world for nearly a decade. With new projects always underway, I don't often reminisce about past projects—quilts that were near and dear to me at the time of their creation but have since been carefully folded and stored on a shelf. Compiling this collection has been a labor of love for me. And an agonizing challenge! Which of my babies should be included?

As I reviewed the many quilts I have designed, memories flooded in. Designing is a fickle process, and there have been many frustrating sewing sessions over the years, long nights when blocks were pushed around in an endless maze of combinations that never seemed right. I cannot count the number of times I have run out of fabric and been unable to find more.

But there have also been many triumphant moments of inspiration, when fabric, color, and shape came together easily and beautifully in perfect harmony. Those are the quilts that are magical—the ones that create themselves.

I'll never forget one late-night design session. My idea, which I thought was brilliant at the time, was to make a Christmas candy quilt from bright red and green Log Cabin blocks. My husband, Mark, entered my sewing room to say goodnight. "Nice watermelon quilt," he commented, studying the blocks on my design wall. I indignantly informed him that it was a Christmas quilt. "No," he responded evenly, "that is definitely a watermelon quilt." He went to bed, and I turned to look at my quilt with new eyes. By morning, I had appliquéd black watermelon seeds all over the quilt, much to my husband's amusement. The result was "Watermelon Picnic," which is one of my most popular patterns and is included in this book (page 53).

I am often asked where I get my design ideas. The question surprises me, because my problem has always been too many ideas and too little time. Even at the movies, I find myself studying the wallpaper on the set rather than listening to the actors. I keep a folder of sketches and photographs that inspire me.

My design whims have evolved over the years. I can never quite settle on one look or style. I love dark reproduction fabrics. I love soft, romantic pastels. I love beautiful, intricate appliqué. I love large, simple patchwork. Like most of you, I have broad tastes that change with my mood. In compiling this collection, I've tried to include a little something for everyone— cheerful berry baskets, elegant appliqué, homespun Christmas projects, and patriotic flags. For those of you who are new to Black Mountain Quilts, I hope you find many projects in this book to inspire you. For longtime readers, thank you for your support. Quilting is my passion and sharing *The Best of Black Mountain Quilts* with you is a joy.

Selecting and Preparing Your Fabrics

Use only high-quality, 100 percent–cotton fabrics for quilting. Cotton fabrics hold their shape and are easy to handle, while blends are sometimes difficult to sew and press accurately.

Developing a Color Scheme

I am frequently asked how I select my colors and prints when I plan a quilt. I call my technique "scrap appliqué" because I like to incorporate as many fabrics as possible. This can be fun and exciting—or a disaster.

The secret to a successful scrap quilt is that although it looks somewhat thrown together, it isn't. It has a deliberate color scheme without looking overly planned.

I usually select two or three fabrics for the main color scheme; for example, "Garden Path," on page 30, began with red, white, and blue. Then I add a lot of similar prints, checks, and solids that are just a touch lighter, darker, or brighter than the main colors. Most of the fabrics in a quilt belong to this second group. In "Garden Path," although I started to develop a group of white prints, the "white" became a single subdued muslin, largely because the reds and blues developed into such large groups that one recurring fabric was needed to frame them.

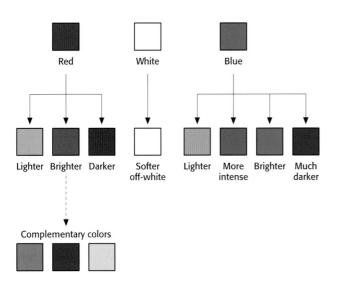

In the third stage, I add contrasting fabrics—fabrics that are much brighter or darker, have white checks or large-scale dots, fabrics in the color complement (opposite on the color wheel), even fabrics that clash. Use them sparingly, but definitely do use them. A whole bolt of electric red-orange fabric may be obnoxious, but when you cut a small round cherry from it and place it on a pale gold background next to a deep red cherry, it appears to be highlighted by sunlight. Used judiciously, contrasting fabrics can keep a quilt from looking flat or dull.

One caveat: When planning your color scheme, keep the finished size of the quilt in mind. Too many contrasting fabrics may overwhelm a small wall hanging, while a large quilt needs more of them to prevent a rigid look.

When you lay out the blocks in rows before sewing them together, look at them and squint. If all the reds look the same, you're using too many similar shades. Be braver! If, on the other hand, the blocks seem to have lost the overall color scheme, tighten things up and use fewer contrasting fabrics (replace some with repeat fabrics, rather than adding more). Many a quilt has been improved by last-minute fabric substitutions—or even remaking a few blocks—before assembling.

Yardage Requirements

Quantities for all quilts in this book are based on 42"-wide fabrics. I assume at least 40" of usable width after preshrinking and specify a minimum width only on a few quilts where it's truly critical.

I frequently suggest that you use a variety of scraps rather than yardage because I like a scrappy look in many of my designs. I often recommend a minimum number of different fabrics for quilters who want a slightly more formal, coordinated look, and a maximum number of different fabrics for those who prefer a scrappier look.

Preparing Fabric for Quilting

Always prewash fabrics to preshrink and test for colorfastness. Never be tempted to skip this step, no matter how eager you are to start cutting those gorgeous fabrics.

Dark colors, bright colors, and light colors should be washed separately. Reds are especially prone to bleed and may require several washings. Don't skimp—wash and rinse until you're certain all the dyes are set, or replace the fabric with another.

Adding a cup of vinegar to the cold rinse water may cure bleeding in some fabrics. Or the staff at your local quilt store may be able to recommend a product that helps set colors.

Press your prewashed fabrics, whether yardage or scraps from your stash, before you begin cutting.

Materials and Supplies

Sewing Machine. You'll need a reliable machine with a good, sturdy straight stitch for piecing. If it has a programmable blanket stitch and other decorative stitches, it will make appliquéing much easier. For machine quilting, a walking foot or darning foot is a must.

Rotary Cutting Tools. Nothing makes patchwork go faster like the right cutting tools. Buy a rotary cutter and cutting mat, plus clear acrylic rulers in commonly used sizes (6" x 6", 6" x 24", 12" x 12", and 15" x 15" will get you started).

Needles. For piecing and appliqué on your machine, a size 70/10 or 80/12 needle works well. If you use a heavier weight thread for the appliqué, choose a machine embroidery needle that has a longer shank to accommodate the thread.

Pins. Straight pins with glass or plastic heads are easy to handle and easy to find. Look for silk pins. They're a little more expensive, but they're exceptionally thin and slide through fabric easily. I use safety pins to baste quilt layers together—just be sure they are rustproof. If you are interrupted and don't get to the quilting right away, you don't want to find that humidity caused the safety pins to rust and ruin your project.

Threads. Use high-quality mercerized cotton thread for piecing, appliqué, and quilting. Save those bargain-table poly/cotton threads for basting. For some applications, I recommend embroidery floss to achieve a certain effect. Again, use the best-quality floss you can buy.

Batting. I use 100 percent–cotton batting, and highly recommend it. I wash my finished quilts to remove markings, then dry them in a warm dryer. The cotton batting shrinks while the preshrunk fabrics don't, resulting in a slightly wrinkled quilt with a vintage appearance.

Scissors and Seam Rippers. You'll need a really good pair of scissors for cutting fabric only. Use another, cheaper pair for template plastic, paper, and cardboard, and keep a small pair of embroidery scissors with sharp blades for snipping threads. A seam ripper will come in handy, too—no one can piece hundreds of blocks without a single mistake!

Markers. I recommend a water-soluble fabric marker throughout the project instructions. The ink from these markers washes out with water. Ask your local quilt shop staff for a recommendation—it's smart to buy one for light-colored fabrics, another for medium, and a third for dark. Obviously, you need to be able to see cutting lines, stitching lines, and other markings, but you also want to be sure that the marks will come out completely. Test your marking tools on the fabrics you're planning to use them on. Make a few solid and dashed lines along the selvages before prewashing.

One note of caution: marks made with some markers may be difficult to remove if you iron over them. If you choose one of the projects in this book that calls for fusible appliqué, test your marker first by marking a scrap, ironing it, then washing it. If your scrap doesn't wash clean, try an ordinary pencil. Mark lightly so you can erase it easily later.

Rotary Cutting

A great time-saver, rotary cutting also makes precision cutting easier. I'll give just a brief overview here. To learn all the ins and outs of rotary cutting, read Donna Lynn Thomas's book *Shortcuts: A Concise Guide to Rotary Cutting* (Martingale & Company, 1999).

1. Match selvages and align crosswise and lengthwise grains as much as you can. Place the fabric on the cutting mat, folded edge next to you. Place a square ruler on the fold, then place

a long ruler to its left. The long ruler should just cover the raw edges of the fabric.

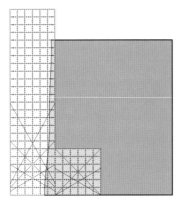

2. Remove the square ruler so you can cut along the right edge of the long ruler. Always roll the rotary cutter away from you. Discard the uneven scrap.

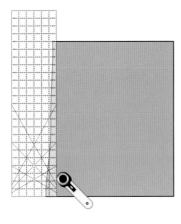

3. To cut strips, align the ruler mark for the required strip width with the fabric edges just squared. Cut along the ruler's edge, rolling the tool toward the selvages.

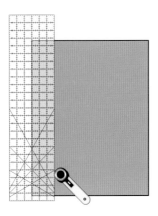

4. To crosscut strips into squares, align the ruler mark for the required measurement with the left edge of the strip. Cut along the ruler's edge. Move the ruler, align it again for the required measurement, and repeat until you have the number of squares needed.

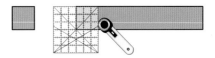

Piecing

All cutting directions in this book include ¼" seam allowances in the measurements for patchwork, blocks, and borders—every piece except appliqués. It is vitally important to maintain an accurate ¼" seam: if five blocks are different in size from the other twenty-five blocks, they won't fit together correctly. If the blocks are all the same size but the size is incorrect, then sashes, borders, and other pieces won't fit properly.

I assume most quilters will piece by machine, but if you piece by hand, mark a light guideline for seams on the fabric and keep a ruler by your side: measure, measure, and remeasure.

Assembly-Line Machine Piecing

To piece by machine, first establish a seam guide exactly ¼" wide. Your machine may have a special foot measuring ¼" from the center needle position to the edge of the foot. Otherwise, create a seam guide by placing a length of tape or moleskin ¼" from the needle, as shown.

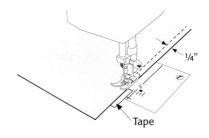

Tape

The fastest way to piece a large number of blocks is to match up identical pieces to be joined at one time. This is often called chain piecing, but I call it assembly-line piecing.

1. Set your machine for 12 stitches per inch. Place the first 2 fabric pieces to be joined under the needle and sew from edge to edge. Stop at the end of the seam, but do not cut the thread.

2. Feed the next 2 fabric pieces under the presser foot, sew from edge to edge, and stop. Feed the next 2 pieces, and so on, without cutting the thread. All seam ends will eventually be crossed by another seam, so there is no need to lock your stitches.

3. When all identical pieces have been stitched, clip the threads to separate them.

Pressing

In quiltmaking, press every seam you sew. The general rule is to press seams to one side, usually toward the darker color. I will occasionally tell you to press seams open because several layers create too much bulk (in "Grandma's Dishes" on page 140, for instance). Unless the directions specify otherwise, press all seams flat from the wrong side, then press them in one direction from the right side. Be careful not to pull or stretch the pieces when pressing.

Appliqué

I use fusible web for the appliqué in all my quilts. It's easy and allows me to work quickly. I trace the templates onto fusible web, iron them to the wrong side of the fabric, cut out the pieces, peel off the paper, and position the pieces. Then I sew over all the edges with a hand or machine blanket stitch or satin stitch, keeping the stitches close together so the quilts will be machine washable.

The directions for all appliquéd quilts specify fusible web. Therefore, the patterns do not include seam allowances and are reversed for tracing onto

fusible web where direction is important. So, remember, if you appliqué by hand without fusible web, you'll need to reverse those templates after tracing them from the patterns. You'll also need to add a seam allowance on all sides.

Making a Template

Use clear or frosted template plastic for durable, accurate templates. Place the template plastic over the pattern and trace with a fine-tip permanent marker. Cut out along the lines and mark the piece name and grain line (if applicable).

Using Fusible Web

Use a good-quality, paper-backed fusible web product. There are many brands on the market; if you haven't already found one that you like, ask the staff at your local quilt shop to recommend a lightweight web for the fabrics you're using. (*Note:* I've calculated the amount of fusible web needed for each project for a 17" width. Some products come in 12" or 20" widths as well, so purchase accordingly.)

All patterns in this book are ready to trace onto fusible web. If appliqué pieces are directional, I've provided a right-side-up diagram to show the placement of appliqués and a group of full-size reversed (mirror image) patterns for tracing onto fusible web.

Manufacturer's instructions vary for different fusible web products, but in general here's the procedure. Try it—it's easy and fast and produces a beautiful quilt. You may never appliqué by hand again.

1. Trace the template outline onto the paper side of the web, repeating for as many pieces as are needed from 1 fabric. (If you need 8 medium pink petals, trace 8 petals onto fusible web.) Cut out the shapes, leaving approximately a ¼" margin all around (not a seam allowance—you'll trim this off in step 3).

2. Fuse all the web shapes to the wrong side of the fabric by pressing.

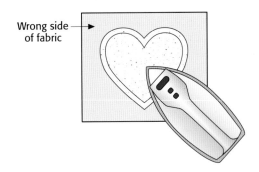

Wrong side of fabric

3. Carefully cut along the traced line. The margin of web makes cutting more accurate.

4. Remove the paper backing only when you are ready to fuse the appliqué to the background. (I often suggest that you experiment first with the placement of your appliqués when a great variety of fabrics are used, to find the best combinations.) Place the appliqué, web side down, on the background and press, following manufacturer's directions.

Right side of background fabric

Right side of appliqué

5. Stitch around all raw edges, except those that will be enclosed in a seam later. This ensures that your quilts will survive machine washing. I usually use a machine blanket stitch, or sometimes a satin stitch, selecting matching thread for a subtle effect, contrasting thread for a folk art effect.

Assembling a Quilt Top

Always take the time to measure and square up completed blocks before assembling them in rows. Use a large square ruler to ensure that the blocks are all the same size and that they are actually the designated finished size, plus ¼" seam allowance.

If there are variations in size among your blocks, trim the largest to match the smallest. Be sure to square them, trimming all four sides, not just one side.

Straight-Set Blocks

To assemble side-by-side rows of blocks, first lay out all blocks and study the quilt for color balance, moving blocks around or making fabric substitutions as necessary. Where block position creates an overall pattern in the quilt, such as in "Autumn Ridge," I recommend numbering the blocks with a water-soluble fabric marker.

1. Sew blocks together into horizontal rows first. Press the seams in row 1 in one direction, in row 2 in the opposite direction, and so on. Alternating the direction of rows reduces bulk where seams meet.

2. Sew the rows together, usually working from top to bottom of the quilt. Match all block seams carefully for vertical alignment.

Follow the same steps if you're using sashes to join horizontal rows of blocks, alternating row 1, sashing strip, row 2, sashing strip, and so on.

Diagonally Set Blocks

I've provided an assembly diagram for all quilts with diagonally set blocks. Again, lay out the blocks with side and corner triangles. Study the arrangement, and move blocks as necessary to achieve the best color balance. Remember, if you need to make fabric substitutions or even remake whole blocks, this is your last chance.

1. Arrange blocks in diagonal rows as indicated in the quilt diagram. Sew the blocks and side setting triangles into rows as indicated. (The triangles will be oversized.) Press seams of alternate rows in different directions.

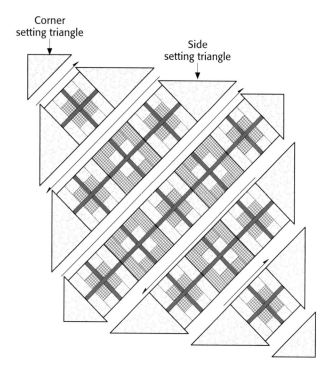

Corner setting triangle

Side setting triangle

2. Sew rows together, matching block seams. Sew corner setting triangles on last.
3. Square up the quilt top, trimming the excess triangle fabric ¼" outside the "points" of the inner blocks.

Adding Borders

All my quilts are designed with straight-cut border corners (no mitering corners for me!). To avoid wavering borders, I always cut border strips to fit the quilt top. Border measurements are included in the "Cutting" section of every project. But since quilts don't always come out exactly the size they're supposed to be (especially large quilts), measure your quilt center before you add the borders. If your quilt center turned out smaller, you can trim your borders. If your quilt center turned out larger, you may have to add additional fabric and then cut to fit.

Here's the way I do it:

1. Measure the length of the quilt top through the vertical center. If it deviates more than ½" from the measurement given in the directions, adjust the side border length before cutting. Cut the side borders. Mark the centers of the quilt sides and the border strips. Pin, matching center marks and ends. Sew in place and press.

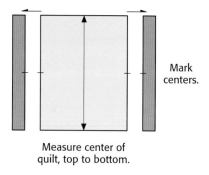

Mark centers.

Measure center of quilt, top to bottom.

2. Measure the width of the quilt top through the horizontal center, including the side borders. Cut the top and bottom border strips, piecing as necessary. Mark the centers of the quilt and border strips. Pin, matching center marks and ends. Sew in place and press.

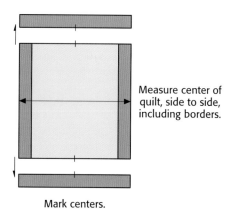

Measure center of quilt, side to side, including borders.

Mark centers.

Wave Good-Bye to Wavy Borders

Ever finish sewing on a long border and find an extra inch of fabric? That's because the feed dogs are pulling the bottom fabric through the machine faster. Sorry, folks, there's no way around it: borders need to be cut to fit and pinned or basted before stitching.

Place the stretchiest fabric (the most loosely woven) on the bottom, next to the feed dogs. And use a walking foot to help feed both layers evenly under the needle. Hold your fabrics gently but firmly, controlling them so they go through the machine at the same speed.

Quilting

If you plan to stitch in the ditch or outline quilt a uniform distance from seam lines, it probably isn't necessary to mark the quilting pattern on your quilt top. However, for more complex quilting designs, you'll want to mark the quilt top before assembling the layers.

Test your fabric marker on a swatch to be sure you can erase it or wash it out. Some quilters like to mark straight quilting lines with masking tape, but don't leave it on your quilt overnight—you may not be able to remove the sticky residue.

Assembling the Layers

Cut your quilt backing at least 4" larger than the quilt top. For large quilts, you'll usually have to piece the backing either lengthwise or crosswise. Press seams open.

1. Spread the backing, wrong side up, on a flat surface. Anchor it with pins or masking tape, being careful not to stretch the backing along the raw edges.
2. Spread the batting over the backing, smoothing out wrinkles.

3. Place the pressed quilt top over the batting, right side up. Make sure the edges are parallel to the edges of the backing fabric.
4. Baste the three layers together. Starting in the center each time, baste diagonally to each corner.
5. Either continue basting in a horizontal and vertical grid or use rustproof safety pins to hold layers in place. Stitching lines or safety pins should be placed in rows 6" to 8" apart.

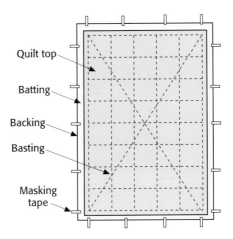

Quilting by Hand

Most quilters use a frame or hoop for hand quilting. Choose the smallest needle you're comfortable using, because it's easier to make small stitches with a small needle. Betweens are a short, sturdy needle favored by quilters.

Aim for small, evenly spaced stitches, drawn firmly through all three layers. An excellent book to help you learn all about hand techniques is *Loving Stitches: A Guide to Fine Hand Quilting* by Jeana Kimball (Martingale & Company).

Quilting by Machine

All of my quilts are quilted by machine, and I highly recommend it. It takes much less time, so you can start another quilt that much sooner.

You'll definitely need a walking foot for straight-line quilting, including stitching in the ditch and outline quilting. This foot is a remarkable help in feeding layers through the machine without shifting or puckering. Your machine may have a built-in walking foot; if not, the staff at your local sewing machine or quilt shop will help you choose the right attachment for your machine.

Walking Foot

Quilting in the Ditch

Outline Quilting

For free-motion quilting, you need a darning foot. Drop the feed dogs on your machine and guide the layers of fabric along your marked design. Use free-motion quilting to stitch around appliqué shapes, to outline quilt a pattern in a print fabric, or to create stippling or curved designs.

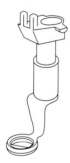

Darning Foot

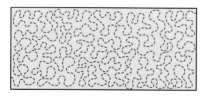

Free-Motion Quilting

Quick Quilting

"Quick quilting," a favorite method of mine for small projects, eliminates binding. First, cut backing and batting slightly larger than your project. Lay the batting out, and center the backing over it, right side up. Center your quilt top over the first two layers, wrong side up. Pin layers together and sew a ¼" seam around the quilt, leaving an 8" opening. Trim excess backing and batting. Clip the corners, turn right side out through the opening, press, and stitch the opening closed. To finish, quilt by hand or machine.

Binding Your Quilt

The binding fabric requirements listed for each quilt in this book are for 2½" strips cut on the straight of grain, as described here.

1. Cut fabric strips 2½" wide. You'll need enough strips to go around the perimeter of your quilt plus 10". Instructions in each project give the number of strips you'll need.

2. Sew strips end to end, right sides together, to make one long strip. Join strips at right angles and stitch diagonally across the corner. Trim and press the seams open.

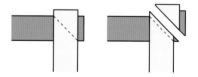

3. Fold the long strip in half lengthwise, with wrong sides together, and press. If you haven't already trimmed backing and batting even with the quilt top, do so now. Also, if you want to add a hanging sleeve (see next section), add it before you bind the edges.

4. Use a precise ¼" seam to attach your binding. Start along one side (not at a corner). Keep raw edges even as you stitch the binding to the quilt top. When you come to the first corner, stop stitching ¼" from the corner and backstitch.

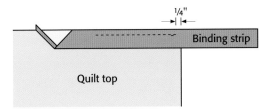

5. Fold the binding up, then back down onto itself, squaring the corner. Turn the quilt 90° under the presser foot. Begin sewing again at the very edge of the quilt top, backstitching to secure the stitches. Continue around the quilt.

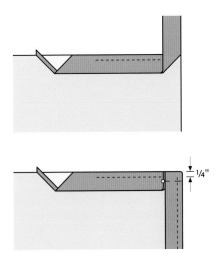

6. When you reach the beginning point, overlap your original stitches by 1" or a little more. Cut away excess binding and trim the end on the diagonal. Tuck the raw edges inside the binding.

7. Fold the binding over the raw edges of all layers. Use a hand or machine blindstitch to sew the binding to the backing.

Making a Hanging Sleeve

A hanging sleeve is a must for any quilt that will be displayed on a wall. Other methods of hanging put a great deal of stress on the fabrics and will shorten the life of your beautiful quilt considerably. It's easy to make a sleeve, and—after all the labor you've invested in your quilt—why wouldn't you?

1. Use fabrics left over from your quilt, or a length of muslin. Cut a strip 6" to 8" wide, about 1" shorter than the width of the top edge of your quilt. Double-fold the short ends (fold under ½", then ½" again). Stitch.

2. Fold the strip in half lengthwise, wrong sides together, and baste the raw edges to the top edge of the back of the quilt. When you add the binding, the edges of the sleeve will be secured and permanently attached.

3. After your binding is complete, finish the hanging sleeve by blindstitching the bottom into position, as shown.

Voilà! Don't forget to sign and date your quilt.

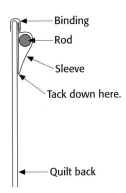

Rose of Tuscany

Finished quilt size: 54" x 68"
Finished block size: 12" x 12"

Materials

Yardage is based on 42"-wide fabric.

2 yds. beige floral print for blocks and outer border

1⅝ yds. plum floral print for inner border

1⅜ yds. medium green for stems and binding

⅝ yd. plum "almost solid" for roses and buds

½ yd. dark green for leaves

4¼ yds. fabric for backing

58" x 72" piece of batting

3 yds. fusible web (17" wide)

Water-soluble fabric marker

Rich plums and romantic mulberry-colored prints ramble over a lush background print. Just as in nature, the colors and textures are layered for lots of interest that captures the eye—and the imagination. While the design looks intricate, the shapes are fused and finished off with machine blanket stitching for a lasting garden of roses.

Cutting

Patterns for the rose, rose center, leaves, stems, and buds are on page 17.

From the plum "almost solid," cut:
12 roses
48 large buds
48 small buds

From the dark green, cut:
96 large leaves
96 small leaves

From the medium green, cut:
48 large stems
48 small stems
7 strips, 2½" x 42"

From the beige floral print, cut:
12 squares, 12½" x 12½"
7 strips, 2½" x 42"

From the plum floral print, cut on the lengthwise grain:
2 strips, 8½" x 48½"
2 strips, 8½" x 52½"

Appliquéing the Blocks

1. Referring to "Using Fusible Web" on page 8, prepare the roses, leaves, stems, and buds for appliqué.
2. With the water-soluble fabric marker, draw placement lines on each of the 12½" beige floral squares. First draw an X through the center of the block, then add horizontal and vertical center lines, as shown.

 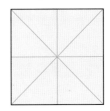

3. Use the placement diagram below to position all the appliqué pieces. Note that the small buds are placed under the stems and the large buds are placed on top of the stems. After fusing the appliqués in place with a hot, dry iron, stitch around the edges of each appliqué to complete the 12 blocks. I used a machine blanket stitch with matching thread.

Placement Diagram

Assembling the Quilt Top

1. Sew the blocks together in 4 rows of 3 blocks each. Press the seam allowances to one side, alternating the direction from one row to the next. Then sew the rows together.

2. Measure the length and width of the quilt through the center. It should measure approximately 36½" x 48½". (If not, see "Adding Borders" on page 10.)

3. Pin and sew the 8½" x 48½" plum floral print strips to the right and left sides of the quilt top. Press seam allowances toward the plum borders. Measure the width of the quilt through the center, adjust the border length if necessary, and pin and sew the 8½" x 52½" plum floral print strips to the top and bottom of the quilt. Press the seam allowances toward the plum borders.

4. Sew 4 of the 2½" beige floral print strips together end to end. From this long strip, cut 2 borders, 2½" x 64½", and sew them to the long sides of the quilt. Then sew the remaining 3 beige floral print strips together end to end. From this long strip, cut 2 borders, 2½" x 56½". Sew these borders to the top and bottom of the quilt. Press.

Finishing

Refer to "Quilting" on page 11 and "Binding Your Quilt" on page 12 for more detailed instructions on finishing techniques, if needed.

1. Piece the quilt backing so it is 4" larger than the quilt top.
2. Layer the quilt top with batting and backing, and baste the layers together.
3. Quilt and bind using your favorite method.

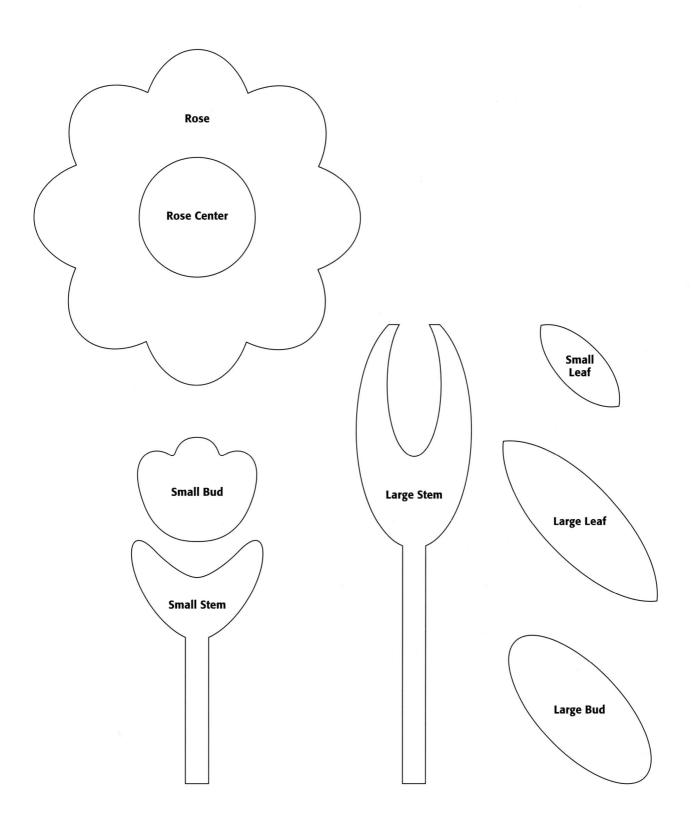

Rose

Rose Center

Small Bud

Small Stem

Large Stem

Small Leaf

Large Leaf

Large Bud

Pink Petals

Finished quilt size: 64½" x 76½"
Finished block size: 12" x 12"

Materials

Yardage is based on 42"-wide fabric unless otherwise stated.

1¼ yds. *each* of 4 off-whites for blocks and borders (off-white group A)

½ yd. *each* of 7 off-whites for blocks (off-white group B)

⅜ yd. *each* of 4 assorted medium to dark pinks for corner border scallops

¼ yd. *each* of 9 assorted medium to dark pinks for side border scallops

¼ yd. brown print for stems and flower centers

1 yd. *total* of assorted medium to dark pink scraps for outer petals and buds

⅜ yd. *total* of assorted light pink scraps for inner petals

⅜ yd. *total* of assorted green and yellow scraps for leaves

⅛ yd. *total* of assorted yellow scraps for bud centers

4¼ yds. fabric for backing

⅝ yd. fabric for binding

68" x 80" piece of batting

6 yds. fusible web (17" wide)

Water-soluble fabric marker

Cutting

Patterns for the petals, flower center, bud, bud center, leaf, stems, and side and corner border scallops are on pages 22–23.

From the assorted medium to dark pink scraps, cut:
48 outer petals
66 buds

From the assorted light pink scraps, cut:
48 inner petals

From the assorted yellow scraps, cut:
66 bud centers

From the assorted green and yellow scraps, cut:
132 leaves

I have a great love for traditional appliqué patterns. I've wanted to make an Ohio Rose quilt for years, but knew I'd be bored using just three or four fabrics throughout, the way this pattern is traditionally made. But what if you created every background block from a different print? And made each flower and leaf a different shade? The result is the warm familiarity of a beloved pattern, yet with the interest of a new approach. And it's so much fun to make!

From the brown print, cut:
12 sets of 4 stems (total of 48)
12 flower centers

From *each* off-white group A, cut:
2 strips, 14½" x 42"
1 square, 12½" x 12½"

From *each* off-white group B, cut:
1 square, 12½" x 12½"

From the 4 assorted medium to dark pinks, cut:
4 corner border scallops (see step 5 of "Making the Border" before cutting)

From the 9 assorted medium to dark pinks, cut:
14 side border scallops (see step 4 of "Making the Border" before cutting)

From the binding fabric, cut:
8 strips, 2½" x 42"

Appliquéing the Blocks

1. Referring to "Using Fusible Web" on page 8, prepare the petals, flower centers, buds, bud centers, leaves, and stems for appliqué. Cut out the centers from the fusible web. The outer petals are medium pinks, with a few dark pinks; the inner petals are light pinks. Buds are mostly medium pinks.

2. On each 12½" off-white block, use the water-soluble fabric marker to draw an X through the center as a guide to position the appliqué pieces.

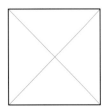

3. Refer to the placement diagram below. Experiment with the placement of individual petals to find the most pleasing arrangement of the assorted pinks against the various off-white fabrics. When you have the most pleasing arrangement of flowers and buds for each block, fuse the appliqués in place. Then stitch around the edges of all appliqués. I used a machine blanket stitch with a mushroom-colored thread to blend in, but you may use another color if you'd like the stitching to stand out.

Placement Diagram

Assembling the Quilt Top

1. Lay out all 12 blocks on your design wall or floor in 4 rows of 3 blocks each, arranging them so that the lighter and darker background fabrics are distributed throughout the quilt (you don't want all the lightest blocks in a clump, for example). Also pay attention to the overall balance of the pink flowers.

2. When you've found the arrangement you like best, sew the blocks together in horizontal rows, then join the rows to complete the quilt center.

Making the Border

1. Measure the length and width of the quilt through the center. It should measure approximately 36½" x 48½". (If not, see "Adding Borders" on page 10.)

2. Each border was cut from a different fabric. You'll need to piece together the two 14½" x 42" pieces from each fabric to create each border. After piecing all 4 border strips, trim 2 of them to the length of your quilt top, which should be 48½". Pin and sew these borders to the long sides of the quilt top.

3. Measure the width of the quilt top through the center. It should now measure approximately 64½". Trim the remaining 2 border strips to this length and sew them to the top and bottom of the quilt top.

4. To cut the side border scallops, trace the side border scallop pattern on page 22 onto template plastic to create half a scallop. Flop the template plastic over and align it with the dashed line. Trace the other half of the scallop to complete 1 side border scallop pattern. Cut out the plastic template and trace around it onto fusible web to make 14 side border scallops. Cut out the centers of the fusible web.

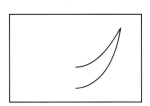

Trace.

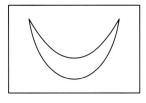

Trace reversed.

5. Use a piece of template plastic at least 12" x 14" to make a template for the corner border scallops. Trace both pieces of the pattern on page 23, joining them along the dashed line to create half a scallop. Flip the plastic to align with the dashed line. Trace the other half of the scallop to complete 1 corner border scallop pattern. Cut out the template plastic and trace around it onto fusible web to make 4 corner border scallops. Cut out the centers of the fusible web.

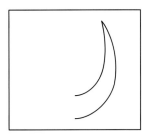

Trace.

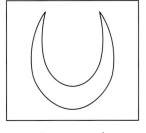

Trace reversed.

6. To help position the scallop appliqués, use the water-soluble fabric marker to draw placement lines. Mark a line across the borders wherever there is a block seam line (as indicated by the blue lines). Mark a short placement line 9" from the outer edge to indicate where the points of the scallops should meet.

7. Prepare the bud and leaf appliqués with fusible web, just as you did for the block appliqués. Position the scallops so that the points meet where placement lines intersect. When you're happy with the arrangement of the various shades of pink, press the scallops in place.

8. Position the buds and leaves at the point intersections and fuse them in place. Stitch around the edges of all appliqués as you did before.

Finishing

Refer to "Quilting" on page 11 and "Binding Your Quilt" on page 12 for more detailed instructions on finishing techniques, if needed.

1. Piece the quilt backing so it is 4" larger than the quilt top.
2. Layer the quilt top with batting and backing, and baste the layers together.
3. Quilt and bind using your favorite method.

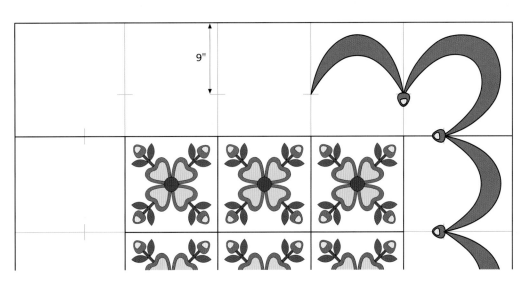

9"

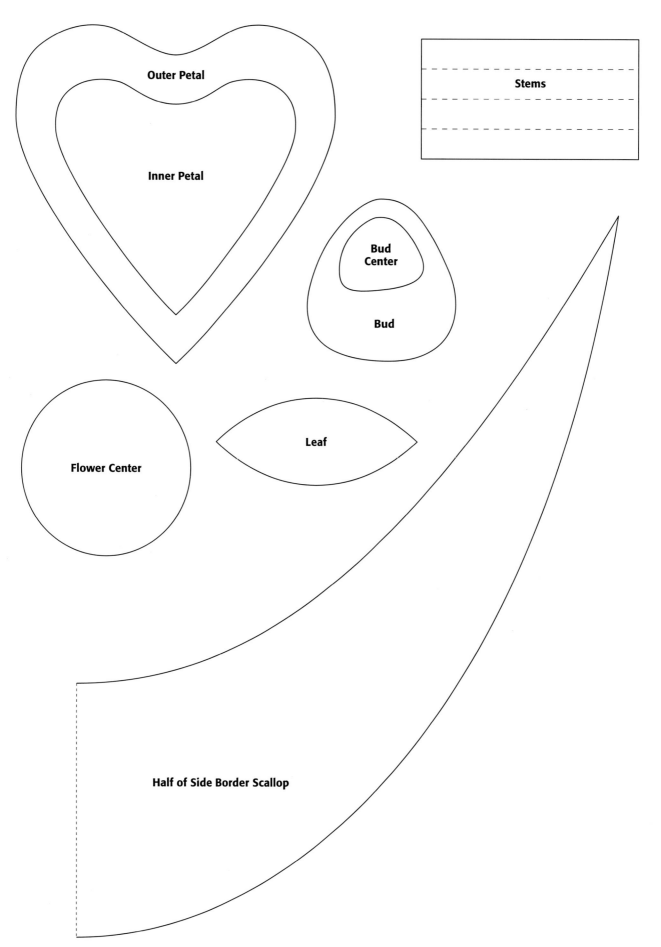

Outer Petal

Inner Petal

Stems

Bud
Center

Bud

Flower Center

Leaf

Half of Side Border Scallop

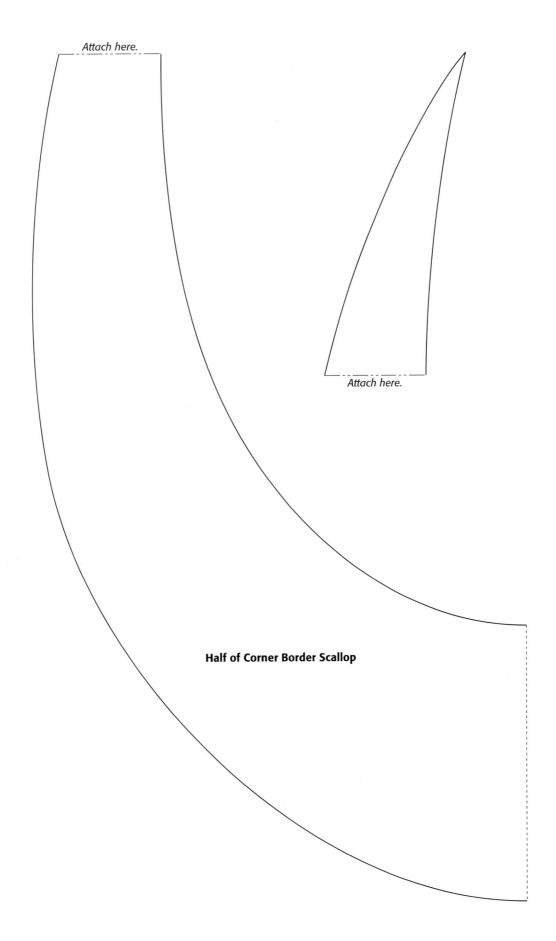

Attach here.

Attach here.

Half of Corner Border Scallop

Tulips and Lace

Finished quilt size: 65" x 55"
Finished block size: 10" x 10"

Materials

Yardage is based on 42"-wide fabric unless otherwise stated.

⅜ yd. *each* of 10 or more assorted white prints for blocks (½ yd. will make 2 blocks)

1⅝ yds. blue print for outer border, leaf motifs, and binding

1⅝ yds. white print for outer border

⅝ yd. muslin for lining tulips

¼ yd. yellow for inner border

¼ yd. brown for stems

⅝ yd. *total* of scraps of assorted yellows for tulips

⅝ yd. *total* of scraps of assorted blues for leaves

3½ yds. fabric for backing

69" x 59" piece of batting

3 yds. fusible web (17" wide)

Water-soluble fabric marker

Cutting

Patterns for the tulip, leaf and leaf motifs, stems, and side and corner border scallops are on pages 28–29.

From the assorted yellow scraps, cut:
80 tulips

From the muslin, cut:
80 tulips; trim them 1/16" smaller than tulip pattern

From the assorted blue scraps, cut:
160 leaves

Pretty yellow tulips growing in a garden of pale blue prints give this quilt the charm of yesteryear. The intricately scalloped border (which isn't at all intricate to do!) adds feminine appeal to this romantic quilt. Why wait for spring to enjoy a bouquet of tulips when you can make your own right now?

From the blue print, cut:
18 side scallops (see steps 1–3 under "Making the Outer Border" before cutting)
4 corner scallops (see steps 1–3 under "Making the Outer Border" before cutting)
4 sets of 3-leaf motifs
18 sets of 2-leaf motifs
6 strips, 2½" x 42"

From the brown, cut:
8 stem units, enough for 40 individual stems

From the ⅜ yd. lengths of assorted white prints, cut:
20 squares, 10½" x 10½"

From the white print for outer border, cut on the lengthwise grain:
2 strips, 7" x 52"
2 strips, 7" x 55"

From the yellow for inner border, cut:
5 strips, 1¼" x 42"

Appliquéing the Blocks

1. Referring to "Using Fusible Web" on page 8, prepare the tulips, leaves, and stems for appliqué. See "Avoid Show-Through" below for a way to prevent show-through by lining appliqués.

Avoid Show-Through

For background blocks, I used fabrics that were mostly white with tiny blue prints. The prints showed through many of the pale yellow fabrics I used for tulip appliqués, so I lined the tulips with muslin, cut 1/16" smaller than the tulips.

To line appliqués, iron fusible web onto both the yellow and the muslin layers. Position a muslin tulip on the background square; then position a yellow tulip over the muslin one. To reduce bulk, cut out the center of the fusible web paper on both layers, leaving about 1/4" around the perimeter of the tulip shape. It's enough to hold the tulips in place without making them stiff.

2. To help position the appliqué pieces on the 20 squares cut from assorted white prints, draw an X through the diagonal center of each using the water-soluble fabric marker.

3. Arrange the tulip design on each block, finding the best combination of background prints, yellows, and blues. When satisfied, fuse the appliqués in place. Then stitch around the edges of all appliqués, using a blanket stitch and matching thread.

Placement Diagram

Assembling the Quilt Top and Inner Border

1. Lay out all the blocks on your design wall or floor, placing them in rows of 5 across and 4 down. When you're happy with the arrangement, sew the blocks together in horizontal rows; then join the rows.

Keeping Things Straight

Once I established the best position, I numbered the blocks 1–20 with a water-soluble fabric marker to keep them in order while I sewed the rows together.

2. To add the inner border, sew 3 of the 1¼" x 42" yellow strips together end to end. From this long strip, cut 2 pieces the same length as the width of your quilt, which should be approximately 50½". Sew these strips to the top and bottom of your quilt. Add the 2 remaining 1¼" x 42" inner border strips to the left and right sides of the quilt.

Making the Outer Border

The lace effect in the outer border is created by appliquéing blue scallops and leaf motifs on a white print border.

White Print Border

Appliqué Scallop and Motif

1. Sew the 7" x 52" white print border strips to the top and bottom of the quilt. Then add the 7" x 55" strips to the short sides of the quilt.
2. To position the scallops accurately, use the water-soluble marker to draw placement lines. Mark the border all the way around the quilt at the points where the tulip blocks are joined, 10" apart (blue lines). Be as accurate as possible.

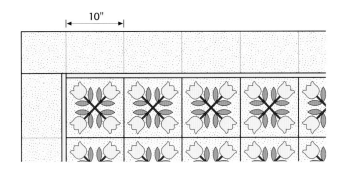

3. Trace 18 side scallops and 4 corner scallops onto fusible web. Iron to the wrong side of the blue print. Cut out the shapes; then peel off the paper.

4. Position the scallops on the outer borders one at a time. Begin by placing a side scallop with one end aligned with the drawn placement line and the overlapping end extending past its placement line by ¼". Press in place.

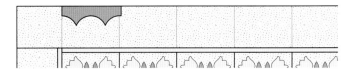

5. Position the next scallop with its edge on the placement line, overlapping the previous scallop. Its other edge should overlap the next placement line by ¼". Iron in place. Repeat, placing and fusing the border scallops around the quilt.

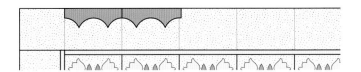

6. Stitch around the curved edges of the scallops, using a blanket stitch. There is no need to sew the outer edges since they will be caught in the binding. I did not stitch the short overlapping ends because I wanted those lines to "disappear."
7. Position the solid blue 2-leaf motifs on alternate scallops, referring to the photograph on page 24 for placement. Press in place. Position the 3-leaf motifs on the corner scallops and press. Stitch around all appliqués, using a satin or blanket stitch and thread in a coordinating color.

Finishing

Refer to "Quilting" on page 11 and "Binding Your Quilt" on page 12 for more detailed instructions on finishing techniques, if needed.

1. Piece the quilt backing so it is 4" larger than the quilt top.
2. Layer the quilt top with batting and backing, and baste the layers together.
3. Quilt and bind using your favorite method.

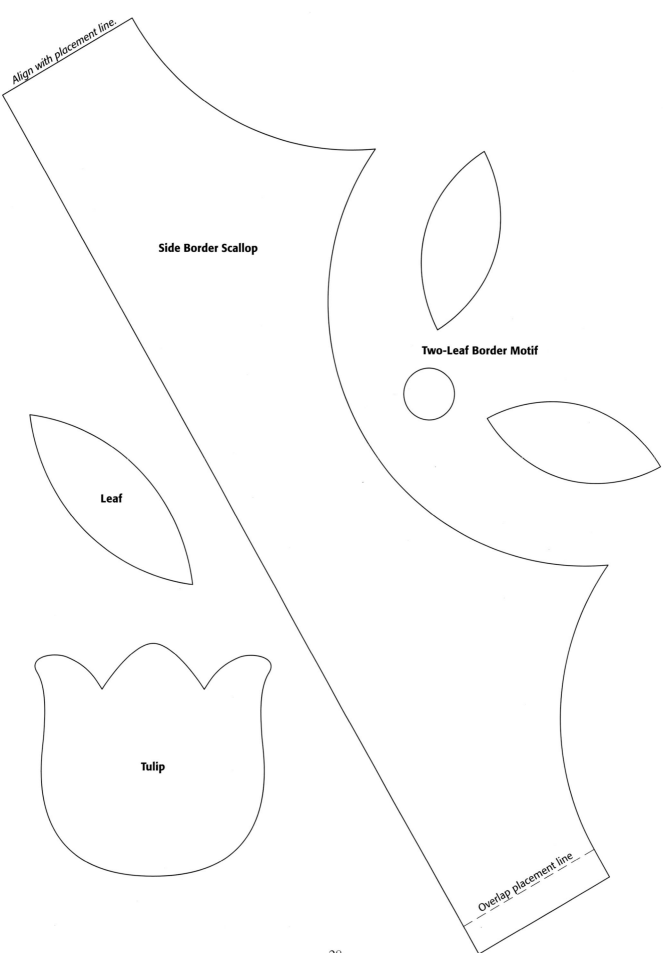

Align with placement line.

Side Border Scallop

Two-Leaf Border Motif

Leaf

Tulip

Overlap placement line

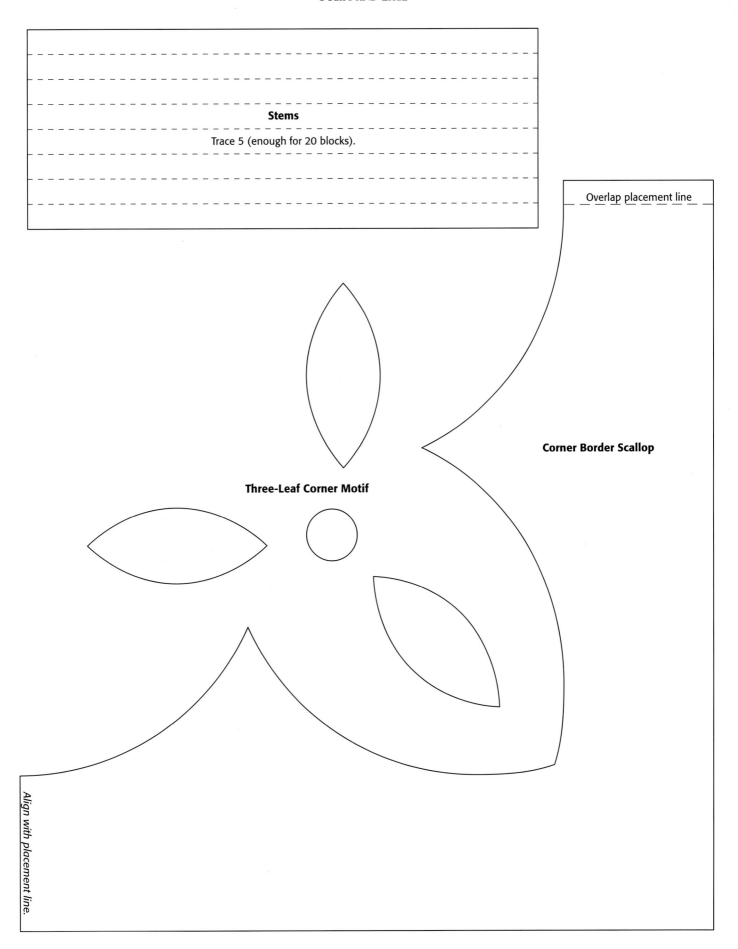

Stems

Trace 5 (enough for 20 blocks).

Overlap placement line

Corner Border Scallop

Three-Leaf Corner Motif

Align with placement line.

Garden Path

Finished quilt size: 52½" x 61½"
Finished block size: 9" x 9"

Materials

Yardage is based on 42"-wide fabric unless otherwise stated.

2¾ yds. unbleached muslin for blocks and middle border

1 yd. blue solid for inner border, outer border, and binding

⅝ yd. *total* of scraps of assorted green prints or solids for leaves

⅓ yd. *total* of scraps of assorted blue prints, plaids, and checks for Stepping Stone blocks

¼ yd. *total* of scraps of assorted reds and pinks for flowers

⅛ yd. *total* of scraps of assorted yellows for flower centers

3 yds. fabric for backing

56" x 65" piece of batting

2 yds. fusible web (17" wide)

Water-soluble fabric marker

Cutting

Patterns for the flower, flower center, and leaf are on page 33.

From the assorted red and pink scraps, cut:
20 flowers

From the assorted yellow scraps, cut:
20 flower centers

From the assorted green scraps, cut:
180 leaves

From the unbleached muslin, cut:
10 squares, 9½" x 9½"
1 strip, 6½" x 42"; crosscut 20 strips, 6½" x 2"
3 strips, 3½" x 42"; crosscut 2 of these strips into 20 squares, 3½" x 3½"; crosscut the remaining strip into 20 rectangles, 3½" x 2"
2 strips, 2" x 42"; crosscut into 40 squares, 2" x 2"
6 strips, 6½" x 42"

In this quilt, two simple blocks are combined to create a charming pattern. Being a fabricaholic, I don't usually make an entire quilt from plain old muslin, but the scrap flowers and scrappy blue blocks seemed to call for a plain background. And after years of tea-dyeing everything, I find the lighter, brighter colors in this quilt very refreshing and pretty.

From the assorted blue scraps, cut:
10 squares, 3½" x 3½"
80 squares, 2" x 2"

From the blue solid, cut:
11 strips, 1½" x 42"
6 strips, 2½" x 42"

Appliquéing the Floral Blocks

1. Referring to "Using Fusible Web" on page 8, prepare the flowers, flower centers, and leaves for appliqué. There are 10 blocks, so you will need 10 flowers, 10 flower centers, and 120 leaves.

2. To help position the pieces on the 9½" x 9½" muslin squares, draw an X through the center of each one with the water-soluble fabric marker.

3. Position a flower in the center of each square, and arrange 4 sets of 3 leaves each along the legs of the X. Place corner leaves ¾" from the edges of the square to allow for seams. The side leaves are tilted slightly toward the corner to help create the overall X shape.

Placement Diagram

4. When you are happy with the appliqué positions, press them in place. Then stitch around all the appliqué edges with a machine blanket stitch. I used black thread to make the flowers really "pop."

Piecing the
Stepping Stone Blocks

1. There are 10 Stepping Stone blocks. For each block you need:
   2 muslin squares, 3½" x 3½"
   2 muslin strips, 6½" x 2"
   2 muslin rectangles, 3½" x 2"
   4 muslin squares, 2" x 2"
   1 blue square, 3½" x 3½"
   8 blue squares, 2" x 2"

2. Sew a 2" blue square to each end of a 6½" muslin strip. Repeat to make a second unit.

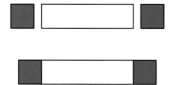

3. Join a 2" blue square to each end of a 3½" muslin rectangle. Then sew a 2" muslin square to each end. Repeat to make a second unit.

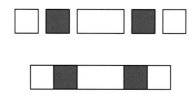

4. Sew 3½" muslin squares to opposite sides of a 3½" blue square.

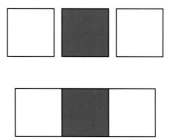

5. Piece the 5 units as shown to complete 1 Stepping Stone block. Repeat to make 9 more blocks.

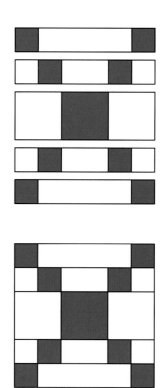

Assembling the Quilt Top

1. Lay out the blocks in 5 rows of 4 blocks each, alternating the Stepping Stone and appliqué blocks. Sew the blocks together in horizontal rows, then sew the rows together.

2. Measure the length and width of the quilt through the center. It should measure approximately 36½" x 45½". (If not, see "Adding Borders" on page 10.) To add the inner border, trim 2 of the 1½" x 42" blue solid strips to 36½" and sew them to the short sides of the quilt.

3. Sew 3 of the 1½" x 42" blue solid strips together end to end. From this long strip, cut 2 strips to 47½". Sew these strips to the long sides of the quilt.

4. To add the middle border, sew 3 of the 6½" x 42" muslin strips together end to end. Repeat to make 2 long strips. Measure the length of the quilt through the center, and from 1 of the long strips cut 2 border strips to this length (it should be approximately 47½"). Sew the strips to the long sides of the quilt.

5. Measure the width of the quilt through the center and cut 2 strips to this length (approximately 50½") from the remaining long muslin strip. Add them to the short sides of the quilt.

6. To add the outer border, sew 3 of the 1½" x 42" blue solid strips together end to end. Cut 2 strips from this long strip to fit the short sides of the quilt (approximately 50½"). Sew the remaining 3 blue solid strips together, then cut 2 strips from them to fit the long sides of the quilt (approximately 61½") and sew them to the quilt.

7. Appliqué 10 flowers and 60 leaves on the middle border, aligning the border flowers with those of the inner blocks and referring to the photograph on page 30 for placement. Stitch around all the appliqué edges with a blanket stitch to match the appliqués on the quilt blocks.

Finishing

Refer to "Quilting" on page 11 and "Binding Your Quilt" on page 12 for more detailed instructions on finishing techniques, if needed.

1. Piece the quilt backing so it is 4" larger than the quilt top.

2. Layer the quilt top with batting and backing, and baste the layers together.

3. Quilt and bind using your favorite method.

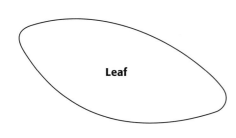

Leaf

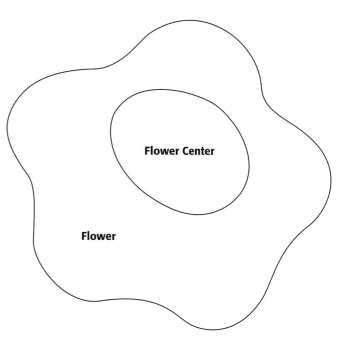

Flower Center

Flower

Posy Patch

Finished quilt size: 50½" x 56½"
Finished block size: 6" x 6"

Materials

Yardage is based on 42"-wide fabric unless otherwise stated.

1¾ yds. unbleached or tea-dyed muslin for blocks and outer border

¼ yd. blue solid for inner border

1⅜ yds. *total* of scraps in assorted colors, prints, stripes, checks, and solids for Nine Patch blocks and appliqués

3 yds. fabric for backing

¾ yd. red solid for binding

55" x 61" piece of batting

2½ yds. fusible web (17" wide)

Cutting

Patterns for the flowers, flower centers, and leaves are on page 36.

From the assorted scraps, cut:
31 large flowers
64 small flowers
95 flower centers
39 large leaves
80 small leaves

From the muslin, cut:
21 squares, 6½" x 6½"
6 strips, 6½" x 42"

From the darker scraps, cut:
105 squares, 2½" x 2½" (cut in groups of 5 for
    coordinated blocks)

From the lighter scraps, cut:
84 squares, 2½" x 2½" (cut in groups of 4 for
    coordinated blocks)

From the blue solid, cut:
5 strips, 1½" x 42"

From the red solid, cut:
6 strips, 2½" x 42"

This quilt has a special place in my heart. I designed it early in my career, when I wasn't sure if I had what it took to be a quilt pattern designer. Its cheerful simplicity made it a bestseller, giving me confidence to go on. The easy Nine Patches and large appliqué shapes make it a perfect project for beginning quilters.

Making the Appliqué Blocks

1. Referring to "Using Fusible Web" on page 8, prepare the flowers, flower centers, and leaves for appliqué. On the flowers and leaves, cut out the centers of the fusible web.

2. On each 6½" muslin square, arrange 1 large flower, 2 small flowers, 1 large leaf, and 2 small leaves, varying placement from block to block.

3. When you're pleased with the arrangements, fuse the shapes in place. Stitch around all appliqué edges. I used a buttonhole stitch and black thread.

Piecing the Nine Patch Blocks

Piece 21 Nine Patch blocks from the assorted 2½" squares. Each block is made of 5 identical dark squares and 4 identical light squares. Sew the squares together in rows, then sew the rows together.

Add a Bit of Whimsy

To create a whimsical look, I occasionally replaced one or two squares with a different fabric (see the photograph on page 34). If you like this effect, you'll need to cut a few extra 2½" squares from scraps.

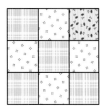

Assembling the Quilt Top

1. Arrange all blocks on your floor or design wall, 6 across and 7 down, alternating appliqué and Nine Patch blocks. Move them around until you achieve a nice color balance. Join the blocks into horizontal rows; then sew the rows together.

2. Measure the length and width of the quilt through the center. It should measure approximately 36½" x 42½". (If not, see "Adding Borders" on page 10.)

3. To make the inner border, sew 3 of the blue solid 1½" x 42" strips together end to end. From this long strip, cut 2 borders, 1½" x 42½", for the long sides of the quilt. Note: If your fabric is wide enough to accommodate this length, you won't have to piece 3 strips together; simply cut 2 strips 42½" long.

4. The width should now be 38½". Trim 2 of the 1½" x 42" blue solid strips to this length (or the width of your quilt top). Sew them to the top and bottom of the quilt.

5. To make the outer border, join 3 of the 6½" x 42" muslin border strips end to end. From this long strip, cut 2 borders the same length as your quilt top (approximately 44½"). Sew them to the left and right sides of the quilt. Repeat, making another long muslin strip. From it, cut 2 borders to the width of your quilt top (approximately 50½"). Join them to the top and bottom of the quilt.

6. Appliqué the border flowers. Arrange 5 flowers and 7 or 8 leaves at each corner, freely mixing large and small flowers and leaves. Use 3 flowers and 5 or 6 leaves along each side. There is no exact placement for the border appliqués: use the photograph for general guidance, but be creative and look for a pleasing color balance with the interior blocks. Fuse the shapes in place, then stitch around the edges as you did on the appliqué blocks.

Finishing

Refer to "Quilting" on page 11 and "Binding Your Quilt" on page 12 for more detailed instructions on finishing techniques, if needed.

1. Piece the quilt backing so it is 4" larger than the quilt top.

2. Layer the quilt top with batting and backing, and baste the layers together.

3. Quilt and bind using your favorite method.

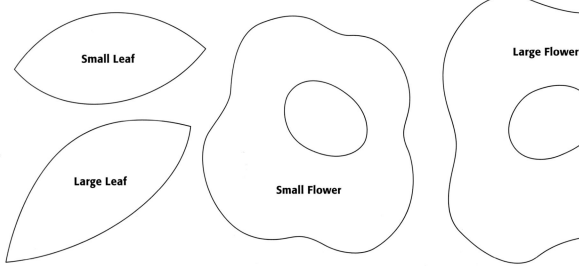

Small Leaf

Large Leaf

Small Flower

Large Flower

Sweet Briar Rose Quilt and Pillowcase

This beautiful quilt is easier to make than you'd imagine. Once the flowers are appliquéd, there are just a lot of long seams to be sewn. The trick is to find the perfect fabric for the sashing and border. A coordinating pillowcase completes the package.

Finished quilt size: 69½" x 94½"
Finished block sizes: 8" x 8" and 20" x 8"

Materials for Quilt

Yardage is based on 42"-wide fabric unless otherwise stated.

4 yds. pink floral print for sashing and outer border

1¾ yds. muslin for appliqué background

1¼ yds. green for sashing, inner border, and binding

¾ yd. pink for sashing

½ yd. purple for sashing

½ yd. brown for stems

⅜ yd. *total* of scraps of assorted greens for appliqués

¼ yd. *total* of scraps of assorted pinks for appliqués

¼ yd. *total* of scraps of assorted lavenders for appliqués

⅛ yd. *total* of scraps of assorted yellows for appliqués

5¾ yds. fabric for backing

74" x 99" piece of batting

3 yds. fusible web (17" wide)

Water-soluble fabric marker

Cutting for Quilt

Patterns for the flowers, flower centers, leaves, and stems are on pages 41–46.

From the green, pink, lavender, and yellow scraps, cut:
6 sets of appliqué pieces 1–24
6 sets of appliqué pieces for daisy A
6 sets of appliqué pieces for daisy B

From the brown, cut:
6 stem pieces 25
6 stem pieces 26

From the muslin, cut:
6 strips, 8½" x 20½"
12 squares, 8½" x 8½"
4 rectangles, 2½" x 8½"

From the pink floral print, cut on the lengthwise grain:
5 strips, 6½" x 56½"
2 strips, 6½" x 82½"
2 strips, 6½" x 69½"

From the green, cut:
20 strips, 1" x 42"
9 strips, 2½" x 42"

From the pink, cut:
15 strips, 1½" x 42"

From the purple, cut:
15 strips, 1" x 42"

Making the Appliqué Blocks

1. Referring to "Using Fusible Web" on page 8, use the patterns (not the placement guide) to prepare all appliqué pieces for the Rose blocks and both Daisy blocks. Because there are so many pieces, write the piece number on the fusible web for each appliqué. It will help you place them later.

2. Using the water-soluble fabric marker, mark placement lines across the center of each 8½" muslin square and each 8½" x 20½" rectangle.

3. Trace the complete rose appliqué design onto the 6 muslin rectangles. Trace the daisy A design (page 45) onto 6 muslin 8½" squares and the daisy B design (page 46) onto 6 muslin 8½" squares, using the water-soluble fabric marker or a pencil. Align the center lines on your muslin and the placement guide carefully.

4. Position the appliqué pieces on each block. When you're satisfied with their placement, fuse the appliqués in place. Stitch around the edges of each appliqué with a matching thread, using a machine satin or blanket stitch.

Assembling the Quilt Top

1. Sew the Rose and Daisy blocks together into rows, alternating placement as shown below. Make 2 rows with roses in the center and 2 rows with roses on the outside. The 2 rows with daisies on the outside and a rose in the center are shorter than the other 2 rows. Sew a 2½" x 8½" muslin rectangle to each end of these rows. All completed rows should measure 56½" long.

2. While the pink floral print strips for sashing are cut on the length of grain and are therefore long

enough for the sashing, the 1½" pink and 1" green and purple strips must be pieced. Cut 5 strips of each color in half to make 10 strips approximately 20" long. Sew each half strip to a matching full strip, to yield 10 long strips of each color. Trim each strip to the same length, 56½".

3. Assemble 7 strips into 1 horizontal sashing unit in the following order: green, pink, purple, pink floral print, purple, pink, green.

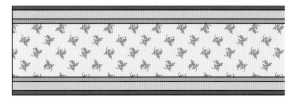

4. Repeat to make a total of 5 horizontal sashing units, joining each as in step 3.

5. Alternating the sashing units with the appliquéd rows, assemble and sew the rows together from top to bottom, starting with a sashing unit.

Adding the Borders

1. Measure the length and width of the quilt through the center. It should measure approximately 56½" x 82½". (If not, see "Adding Borders" on page 10.) As with the sashing, the outer border strips have been cut lengthwise to fit. The green inner borders will need to be pieced.

2. Sew together 5 of the green 1" strips end to end. From this long strip, cut 2 side borders, 1" x 82½" (or the length of your quilt). Sew them to the sides of the quilt.

3. To make the outer border, sew the 6½" x 82½" pink floral print border strips to the quilt sides. Then add the 6½" x 69½" floral border strips to the top and bottom of the quilt.

Finishing

Refer to "Quilting" on page 11 and "Binding Your Quilt" on page 12 for more detailed instructions on finishing techniques, if needed.

1. Piece the quilt backing so it is 4" larger than the quilt top.

2. Layer the quilt top with batting and backing, and baste the layers together.

3. Quilt and bind using your favorite method.

Materials for Pillowcase

Yardage is based on 42"-wide fabric unless otherwise stated.

1⅝ yds. floral print

⅞ yd. muslin

¼ yd. brown for stems

⅛ yd. purple for trim

Scraps of assorted pinks and greens for appliqué

Water-soluble fabric marker

Cutting for Pillowcase

Patterns for the flowers, flower centers, stems, and leaves are on pages 41–44; they are the same as those used in the Sweet Briar Rose quilt.

From the muslin, cut:
1 rectangle, 16½" x 20½"

From the purple, cut:
1 strip, 1½" x 20½"

From the floral print, cut:
1 rectangle, 20½" x 36½"
1 rectangle, 20½" x 19½"

Making the Pillowcase

1. Referring to "Using Fusible Web" on page 8, prepare 2 roses, leaves, and stems for appliqué, pieces 1–26.
2. Using the water-soluble fabric marker, draw placement guidelines on the muslin rectangle. Draw a line 4¼" away from one long edge. Then draw a second line perpendicular to the first through its midpoint, as shown.

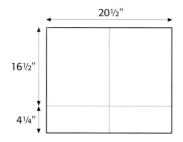

3. Referring to the placement guides on pages 43–44 and using the marked guidelines, position the appliqué pieces on the muslin fabric. When you are satisfied with their placement, remove the paper backing and fuse in place. Using matching thread, stitch around the outer edges of each shape with a machine blanket stitch.
4. Sew the 1½" x 20½" purple strip to the bottom of the appliquéd fabric. The band should be closest to the appliqué, not at the other end. Press the seam allowance toward the muslin.
5. Sew the 20½" x 19½" floral print rectangle to the opposite side of the purple trim.
6. On both the muslin end of pillowcase front from step 5 and on the pillowcase back (the 20½" x 36½" floral print rectangle), press under ¼" along the end. Then fold under 8" of fabric to serve as a facing. Stitch along the edge folded under to secure the facing. On the pillowcase front, this stitching will serve as topstitching about 1/16" above the purple trim.

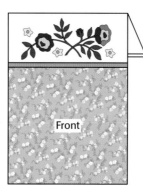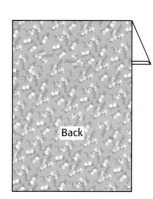

Fold under 8".

7. Pin the pillowcase front to the back, right sides together. Sew along the sides and bottom, using a ¼" seam allowance. (Be sure to leave the top open!) Clip the bottom corners; then finish the seam edges using a machine zigzag or overcast stitch.

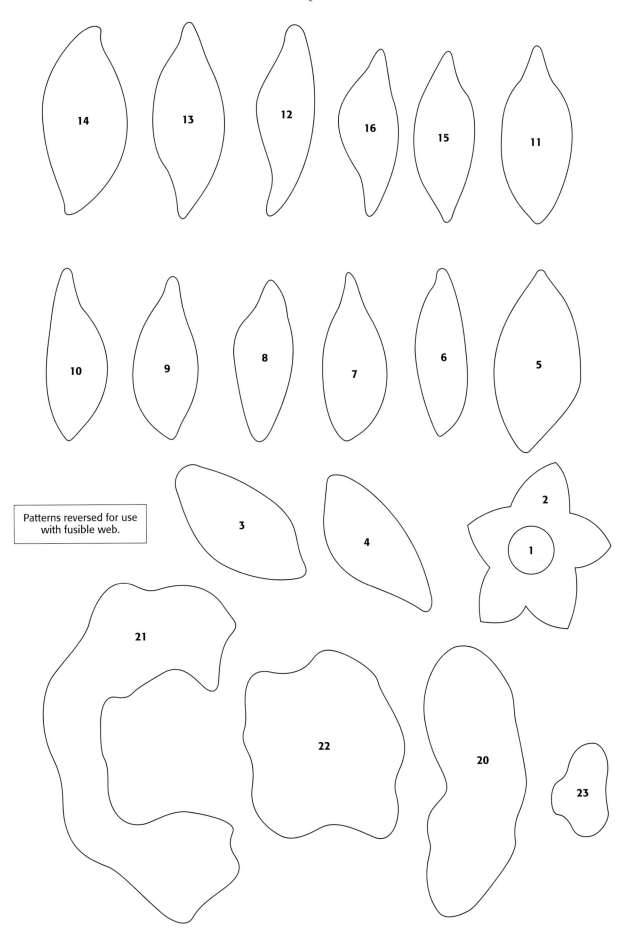

Patterns reversed for use
with fusible web.

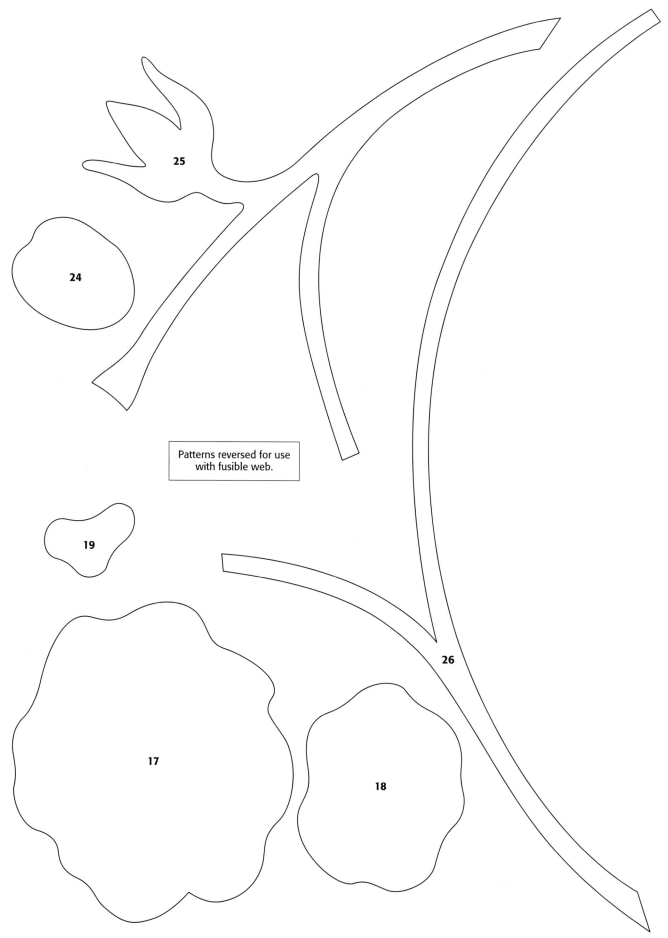

Patterns reversed for use
with fusible web.

25

24

19

26

17

18

10

26

9

8

7

6

2

1

Placement Guide
Right side up for tracing
onto background fabric

17

18

19

2

1

5

4

3

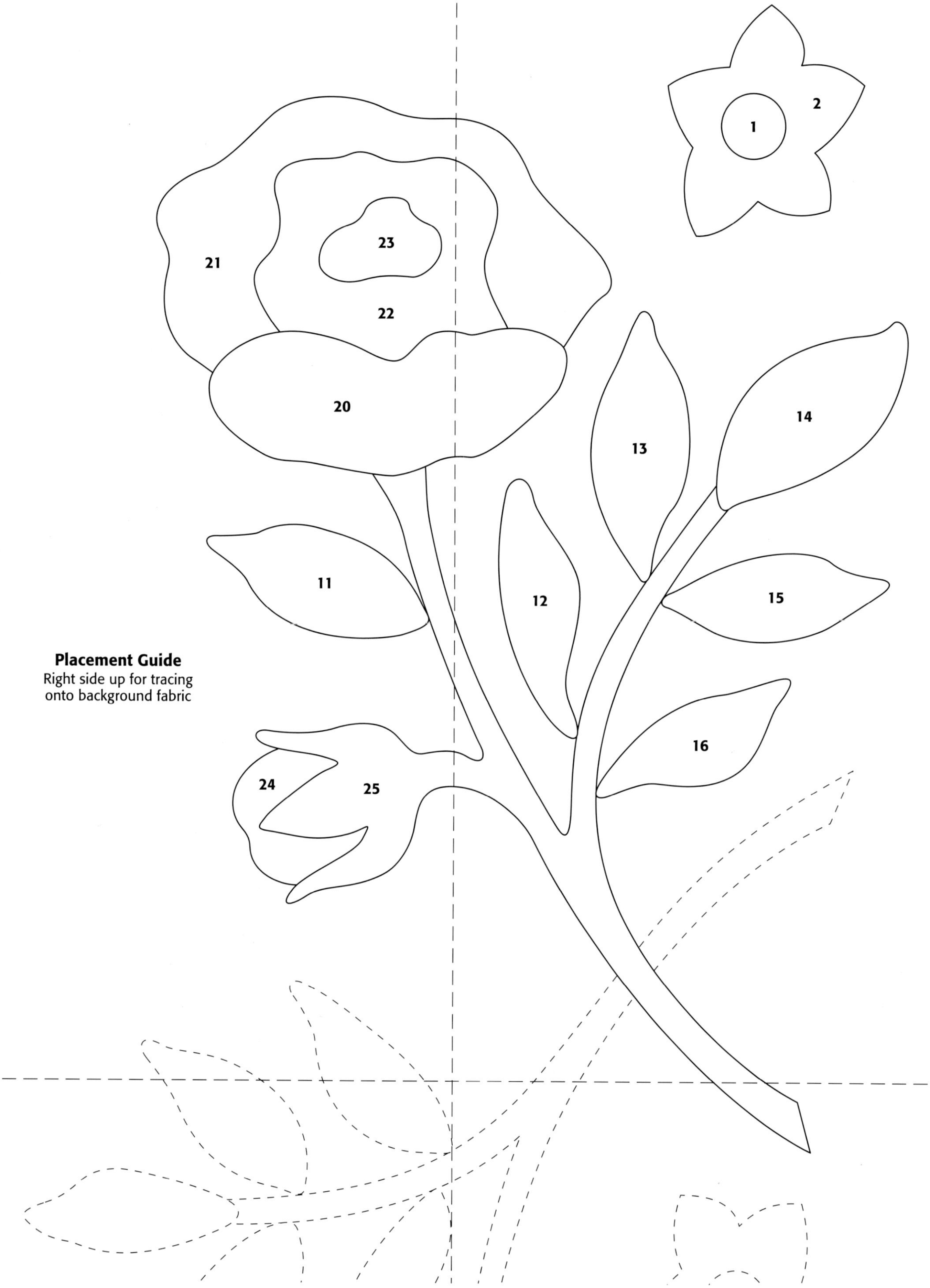

2

1

21

23

22

20

13

14

11

15

12

Placement Guide
Right side up for tracing
onto background fabric

16

24   25

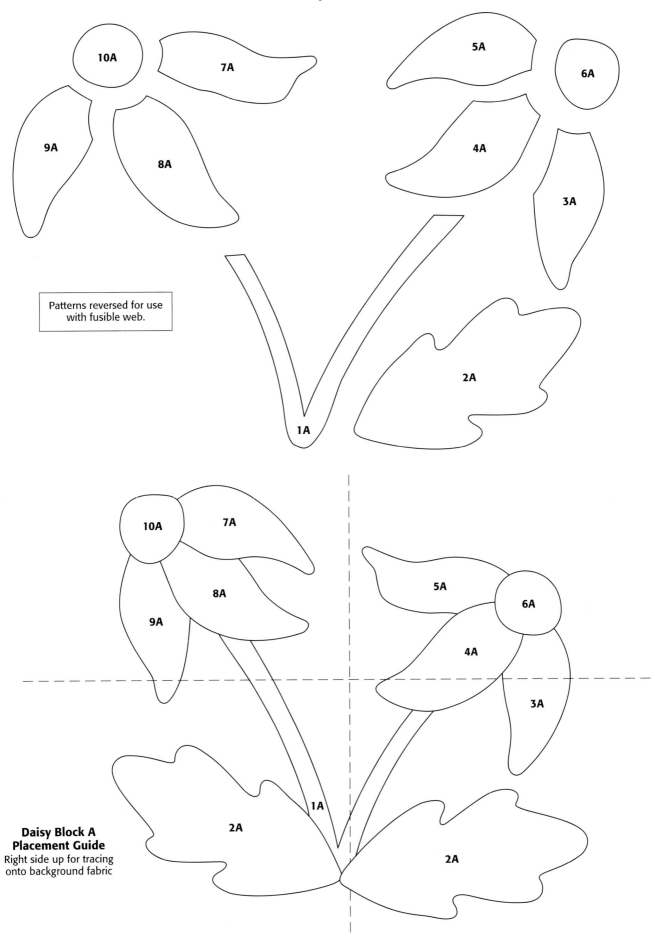

10A

7A

9A

8A

5A

6A

4A

3A

Patterns reversed for use
with fusible web.

2A

1A

10A

7A

8A

9A

5A

6A

4A

3A

**Daisy Block A
Placement Guide**
Right side up for tracing
onto background fabric

1A

2A

2A

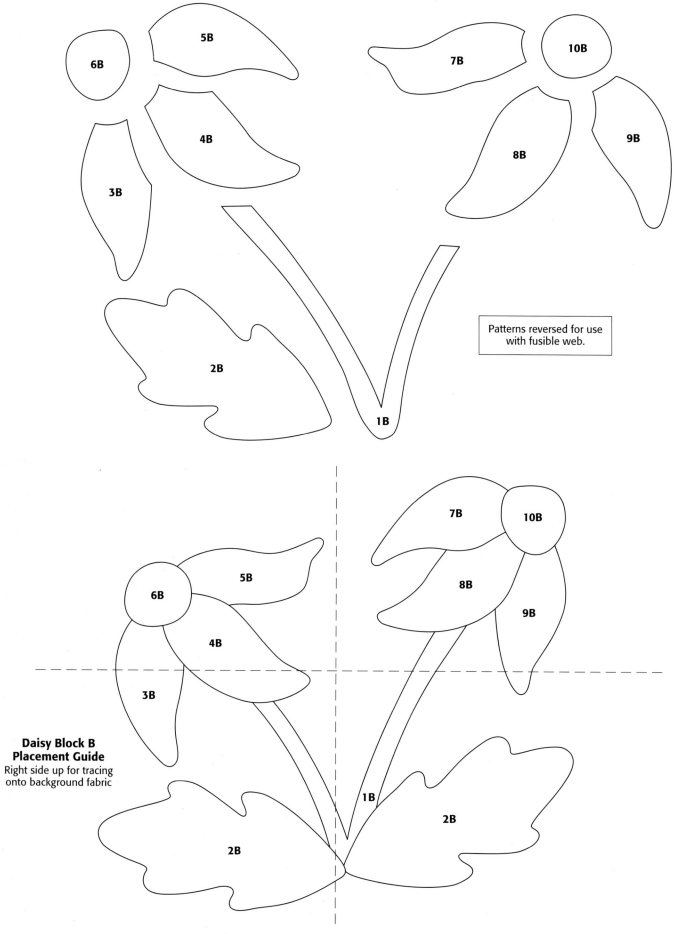

6B

5B

7B

10B

4B

8B

9B

3B

Patterns reversed for use
with fusible web.

2B

1B

7B

10B

5B

8B

6B

9B

4B

3B

**Daisy Block B
Placement Guide**
Right side up for tracing
onto background fabric

1B

2B

2B

Posy Baskets

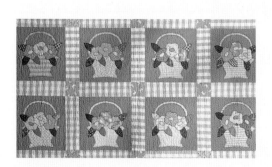

Depression-era-green backgrounds mixed with assorted pastel appliqués and a large-scale check make "Posy Baskets" a perfect fit for a cottage-style decor. Atop an old iron bed, draped on the back of your favorite reading chair, or trailing out of a basket, this charming quilt is sure to add just the right touch of nostalgia to your room.

Finished quilt size: 79½" x 79½"
Finished block size: 11" x 11"

Materials

Yardage is based on 42"-wide fabric unless otherwise stated.

3¾ yds. light plaid or check for sashing and middle border

3½ yds. green solid for blocks, inner and outer borders, and binding

⅜ yd. pink print for sashing squares

10" square *each* of 16 light prints for baskets

½ yd. *total* of scraps of assorted green prints, plaids, solids, and checks for leaves

½ yd. *total* of scraps of assorted pink, blue, purple, and yellow prints, plaids, solids, and checks for posy appliqués

4⅞ yds. fabric for backing

84" x 84" piece of batting

4½ yds. fusible web (17" wide)

Cutting

Patterns for the basket, posy, posy center, and leaf are on pages 50–51.

From the light prints, cut:
16 baskets

From the assorted pink, blue, purple, and yellow scraps, cut:
48 posies
48 posy centers

From the assorted green scraps, cut:
80 leaves

From the green solid, cut:
16 squares, 11½" x 11½"
14 strips, 1½" x 42"
9 strips, 2½" x 42"

From the pink print, cut:
3 strips, 3½" x 42"; crosscut into 25 squares, 3½" x 3½"

From the light plaid or check, cut:
14 strips, 3½" x 42"; crosscut into 40 strips, 3½" x 11½"
2 strips, 8½" x 61½", cut on the lengthwise grain
2 strips, 8½" x 77½", cut on the lengthwise grain

Making the Basket Blocks

1. Referring to "Using Fusible Web" on page 8, prepare the baskets, posies, posy centers, and leaves for appliqué. On the large pieces, cut out the center of the fusible web.

2. Arrange 1 basket, 3 posies and 3 posy centers, and 5 leaves on each 11½" green solid background square. Mix and match pink, blue, purple, and yellow flowers with a variety of green leaves.

3. When you have the appliqués arranged to your satisfaction, fuse the shapes in place, then stitch around the edges of all appliqués with a machine blanket stitch to complete 16 blocks.

Placement Diagram

A Thread That's Just Right

After making a sample block using a black buttonhole stitch around the appliqués, I determined it was too dark for the pastels of this quilt. So I tried a mushroom-colored thread, which was too light. The sample I liked best was an olive green thread, which I used throughout this quilt. Experiment on scraps of your fabrics to find the effect you like best.

Assembling the Quilt Top

1. Alternating the 3½" pink print squares and the 3½" x 11½" light plaid or check strips, assemble and stitch 5 horizontal sashing rows.

Make 5.

2. Join the Basket blocks into 4 rows of 4 blocks each. Alternate the Basket blocks with the remaining 3½" x 11½" sashing strips.

Make 4.

3. Starting with a sashing row, and alternating basket rows with sashing rows, sew the quilt top together from top to bottom.

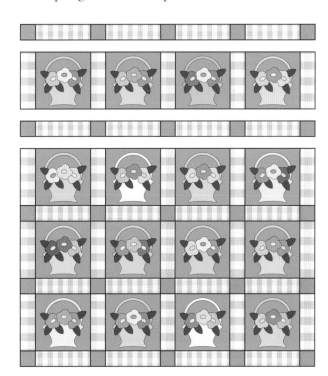

Adding the Borders

1. Measure your quilt through the center in both directions. It should measure approximately 59½" x 59½". (If not, see "Adding Borders" on page 10.)

2. To make the inner border, sew 3 of the 1½" x 42" green solid strips together end to end. From this long strip, cut 2 borders, 1½" x 59½". Sew them to the left and right sides of the quilt. Repeat for the top and bottom borders, this time cutting 2 borders 1½" x 61½". If 3 strips of your fabric sewn together aren't long enough for the 2 borders, you may need to piece together 4 strips.

3. To make the middle border, sew the 8½" x 61½" light plaid or check border strips to the left and right sides of the quilt. Then sew the 8½" x 77½" border strips to the top and bottom of the quilt.

4. To make the green outer border, sew together two 1½" x 42" strips end to end. Repeat. From each long strip, cut a 1½" x 77½" green border and sew them to the sides of the quilt. Repeat for the top and bottom borders, cutting them 79½" long. Sew them to the top and bottom of the quilt.

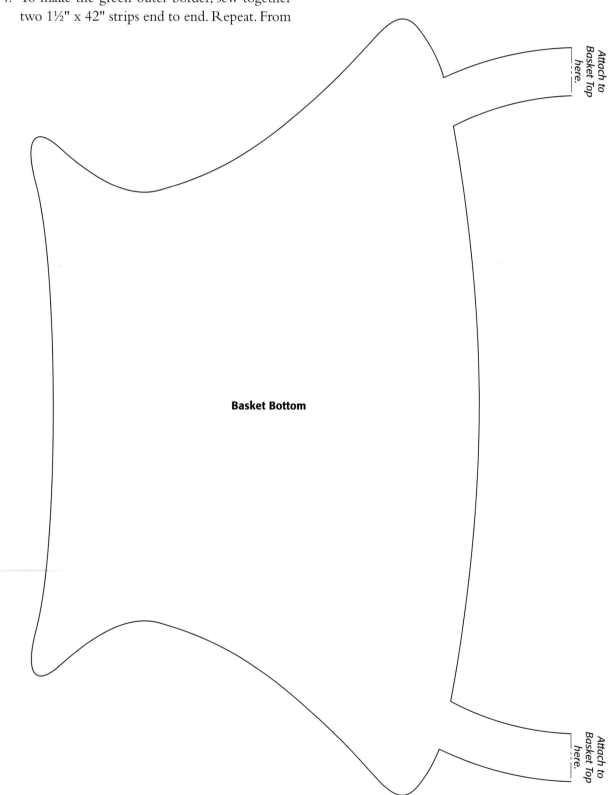

Attach to Basket Top here.

Basket Bottom

Attach to Basket Top here.

Finishing

Refer to "Quilting" on page 11 and "Binding Your Quilt" on page 12 for more detailed instructions on finishing techniques, if needed.

1. Piece the quilt backing so it is 4" larger than the quilt top.

2. Layer the quilt top with batting and backing, and baste the layers together.

3. Quilt and bind using your favorite method.

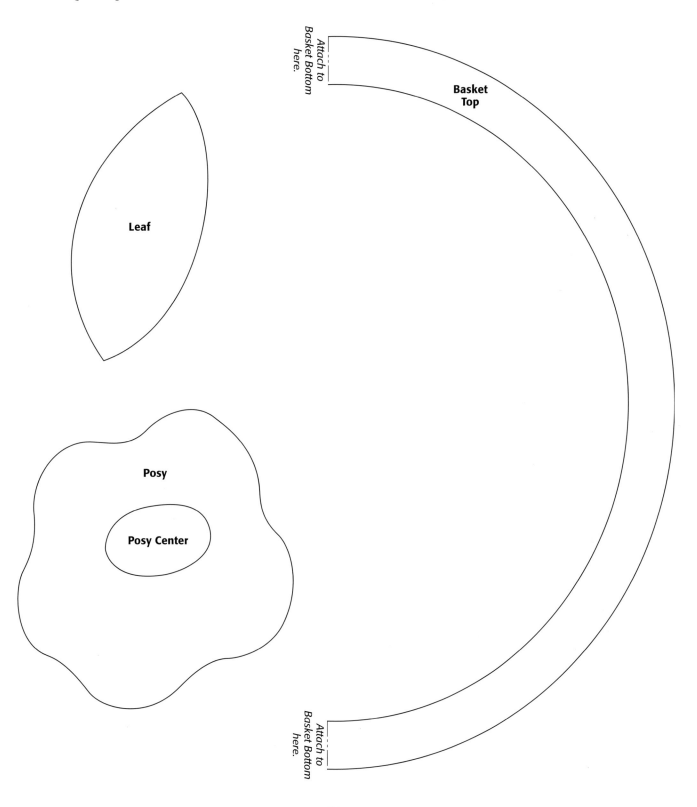

Watermelon Picnic

Finished quilt size: 52½" x 60"
Finished block size: 7½" x 7½"

Materials

Yardage is based on 42"-wide fabric.

1½ yds. *total* of assorted ivory prints

1 yd. *total* of assorted red prints and ginghams

1 yd. *total* of assorted green prints and checks

¼ yd. black solid for watermelon seeds

3¼ yds. fabric for backing

½ yd. dark green for binding

57" x 64" piece of batting

⅓ yd. fusible web (17" wide)

Cutting

The pattern for the watermelon seeds is on page 55.

From the red prints, cut:
28 squares, 2" x 2"
28 rectangles, 2" x 3½"
28 rectangles, 2" x 5"
28 strips, 2" x 6½"
28 strips, 2" x 8"

From the ivory prints, cut:
56 squares, 2" x 2"
56 rectangles, 2" x 3½"
56 rectangles, 2" x 5"
56 strips, 2" x 6½"

From the green prints, cut:
28 squares, 2" x 2"
28 rectangles, 2" x 3½"
28 rectangles, 2" x 5"
28 strips, 2" x 6½"
28 strips, 2" x 8"

From the black solid, cut:
84 watermelon seeds

From the dark green, cut:
6 strips, 2½" x 42"

Our lives are filled with special days, from birthdays and holidays to less fixed occasions that nevertheless engrave themselves in our memories. Make a picnic by the lake or an impromptu meal in the backyard all the more special with this "Watermelon Picnic" quilt. Or, if you don't want to use a quilt outdoors, perk up your indoor decor with the feeling of summer and biting into the first juicy slice of red, ripe watermelon.

Piecing the Log Cabin Blocks

This enchanting quilt is constructed from 56 Log Cabin blocks: 28 red-and-ivory blocks and 28 green-and-ivory blocks. All blocks are pieced and sewn the same way. The cutting directions at left give the exact number of pieces needed, but you may need to cut more in order to adjust colors as you work. Keep the strips organized by color and length.

1. Assemble the pieces for 1 Log Cabin block. You'll need:

   1 red or green 2" x 2" square
   1 red or green 2" x 3½" rectangle
   1 red or green 2" x 5" rectangle
   1 red or green 2" x 6½" strip
   1 red or green 2" x 8" strip
   1 ivory 2" x 2" square
   1 ivory 2" x 3½" rectangle
   1 ivory 2" x 5" rectangle
   1 ivory 2" x 6½" strip

2. To make a red-and-ivory block, sew a 2" ivory square to a 2" red square. Press the seam allowance toward the red fabric.

3. Add a 2" x 3½" ivory strip to the right side of the unit. Press the seam allowances (and all the rest of the seam allowances) toward the newest strip.

4. Rotate the block a quarter-turn clockwise and add a 2" x 3½" red strip to the unit. Rotate another quarter turn and add a 2" x 5" red strip to the block.

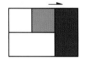

5. Continue rotating the block and adding strips. The next 2 strips will be ivory, followed by 2 more red strips to complete the block. The finished block should measure 8" x 8".

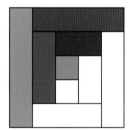

6. Repeat steps 1–5 to make a total of 28 red-and-ivory blocks. Then repeat, substituting the green squares and strips to make 28 green-and-ivory blocks.

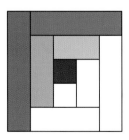

Mix 'em Up!

I suggest sewing five red blocks and five green blocks to start. Lay them out to see how they look together. Do you need more dark greens? Or perhaps larger-scale prints? Is your combination of reds achieving that "watermelon" illusion? Cut strips of different fabrics if necessary. Then continue sewing until all blocks are finished.

Assembling the Quilt Top

1. Referring to "Using Fusible Web" on page 8, prepare the watermelon seeds for appliqué. Appliqué 3 black solid seeds on each of the red Log Cabin blocks as shown in the photo on page 52.
2. Lay out the Log Cabin blocks, 7 across and 8 down, referring to the assembly diagram for color placement. The first row will be: 2 red, 2 green, 2 red, 1 green. Change the orientation of every other block by 180° to create the diagonal color bands.

3. Review the color placement and take time to rearrange blocks as necessary to achieve the best color bands. In certain configurations, the ivories will create a sunshine-to-shade illusion and the dark greens will take on a "watermelon rind" effect.
4. Sew the blocks together in horizontal rows. It's important to keep all blocks in the correct location and orientation, so you may want to number the blocks by using adhesive dots or by writing on the backs with a water-soluble fabric marker.

5. Join the horizontal rows. Recheck the position of the color bands as you work.

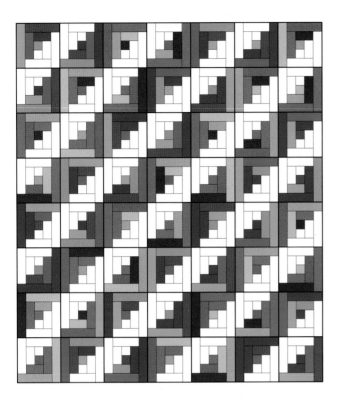

Finishing

Refer to "Quilting" on page 11 and "Binding Your Quilt" on page 12 for more detailed instructions on finishing techniques, if needed.

1. Piece the quilt backing, using a horizontal seam. Trim it so it is 4" larger than the quilt top.

2. Layer the quilt top with batting and backing, and baste the layers together.

3. Quilt and bind using your favorite method.

Watermelon Seeds
Trace 14 times onto fusible web
to create 84 seeds, enough for 28 blocks.

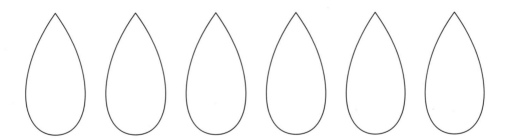

Blueberry Baskets

Finished quilt size: 33" x 19"
Finished block size: 6½" x 9½"

Materials

Yardage is based on 42"-wide fabric unless otherwise stated.

¼ yd. (or fat quarter) *each* of 3 medium golds for baskets

½ yd. light gold print for sashing and border

⅜ yd. blue print for border and binding

¼ yd. light print for blocks

Scraps of blues and greens for blueberries and leaves

¾ yd. fabric for backing

23" x 37" piece of batting

½ yd. fusible web (17" wide)

Cutting

Patterns for the basket, blueberry, and leaf are on page 59.

From *each* of the 3 medium golds, cut:
1 basket

From the blue scraps, cut:
6 blueberries

From the green scraps, cut:
9 leaves

From the light print, cut:
3 rectangles, 7" x 10"

From the light gold print, cut:
4 strips, 2½" x 10"
2 strips, 2½" x 28"
2 strips, 2½" x 15"
2 strips, 2½" x 33"

From the blue print, cut:
2 strips, 1" x 14"
2 strips, 1" x 29"
3 strips, 2½" x 42"

Blueberry muffins, blueberry buckle, blueberry pie, blueberries topped with whipped cream … there are so many ways to enjoy eating blueberries in the summertime. Here are two fresh ways to use this delectable fruit in quilts: Blueberry Baskets (instructions begin on this page) and Blueberry Wreath (instructions begin on page 60). Calorie-free and loads of fun, I can't think of a better way to enjoy blueberries year round.

Making the Blocks

1. Referring to "Using Fusible Web" on page 8, prepare the baskets, blueberries, and leaves for appliqué. On the basket pieces, cut out the center of the fusible web.

2. Arrange the baskets, blueberries, and leaves on the 7" x 10" light print blocks. I positioned the blueberries and leaves a little differently in each basket. Play with the appliqué pieces until you're pleased with all 3 blocks.

3. Fuse the appliqués in place, then machine stitch around their edges using matching thread and a blanket or satin stitch.

Assembling the Quilt Top

1. Join the 3 Basket blocks and four 2½" x 10" light gold sashing strips, side by side. Press the seam allowances toward the sashing strips.

2. Sew the 2½" x 28" light gold print border strips to the top and bottom of the quilt.

3. Sew the 1" x 14" blue print border strips to the quilt sides. Sew the 1" x 29" blue print border strips to the top and bottom of the quilt. Press all seam allowances toward the blue borders.

4. Sew the 2½" x 15" light gold print border strips to the quilt sides. Sew the 2½" x 33" light gold borders to the top and bottom of the quilt. Press the seam allowances toward the light gold print borders.

Finishing

Refer to "Quilting" on page 11 and "Binding Your Quilt" on page 12 for more detailed instructions on finishing techniques, if needed.

1. Trim the quilt backing so it is 4" larger than the quilt top.

2. Layer the quilt top with batting and backing, and baste the layers together.

3. Quilt and bind using your favorite method.

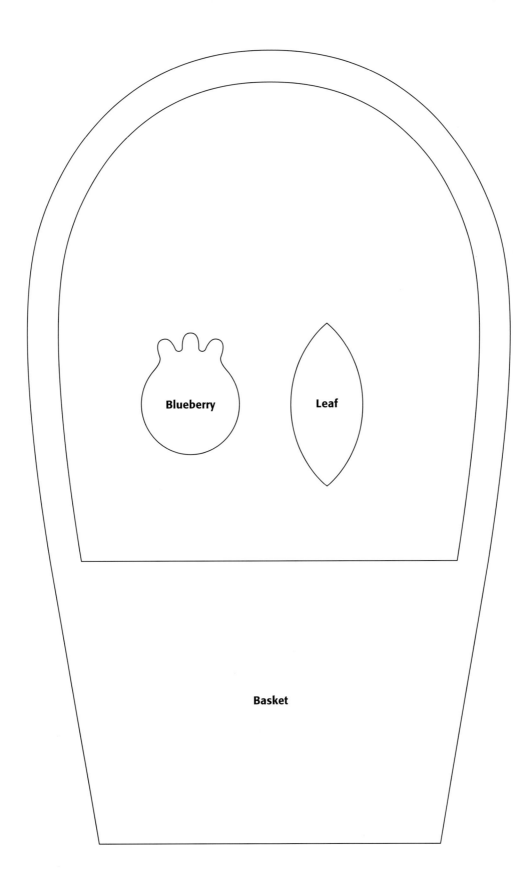

Blueberry

Leaf

Basket

Blueberry Wreath

Finished quilt size: 41½" x 41½"
Finished block size: 10" x 10"

Materials

Yardage is based on 42"-wide fabric.

2 yds. light print for block backgrounds and borders

1¼ yds. green print for wreaths, leaves, borders, and binding

⅛ yd. blue print for blueberries

2½ yds. fabric for backing★

45" x 45" piece of batting

1¼ yds. fusible web (17" wide)

Water-soluble fabric marker

★*Note: If your backing fabric is 44" wide, you can purchase just 1⅜ yards of fabric. However, many fabrics are narrower than that and you'll need two lengths of fabric to piece the backing.*

Cutting

Patterns for the wreath, leaf, and blueberry are on page 63.

From the green print, cut:
4 wreaths
96 leaves
8 strips, 1" x 10½"
8 strips, 1" x 11½"
2 strips, 1" x 32½"
2 strips, 1" x 33½"
5 strips, 2½" x 42"

From the blue print, cut:
96 blueberries

From the light print, cut:
4 squares, 10½" x 10½"
2 strips, 2½" x 11½"
1 strip, 2½" x 24½"
2 strips, 4½" x 24½"
2 strips, 4½" x 32½"
2 strips, 4½" x 33½"
2 strips, 4½" x 41½"

Making the Wreath Blocks

1. Referring to "Using Fusible Web" on page 8, prepare the wreaths, leaves, and blueberries for appliqué.
2. With the water-soluble fabric marker, draw diagonal placement lines on the right sides of the four 10½" light print squares.

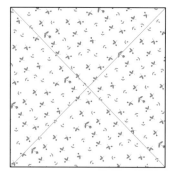

3. Referring to the placement diagram below, arrange the wreath, leaves, and blueberries on each block. First, fuse the wreath in place; then position the blueberries, centering them on the diagonal placement lines. Last, fill in the gaps with leaves, making sure they are facing the same direction on all 4 blocks (mine all face clockwise). After fusing, stitch around the outside edges of all appliqués using a machine blanket stitch and matching thread.

Placement Diagram

Joining Blocks and Sashing

1. Sew the 1" x 10½" green print strips to the right and left sides of all 4 appliqué blocks.

2. Stitch the 1" x 11½" green print strips to the top and bottom of each block.

3. Join 2 appliquéd blocks to either long side of a 2½" x 11½" light print sashing strip. Repeat to make 2 such rows.

Make 2.

4. Join the 2 rows with the 2½" x 24½" light print sashing strip in the middle, as shown.

61

Adding the Borders

1. Position, pin, and sew the 4½" x 24½" light print border strips to the sides of the block unit. Then position, pin, and sew the 4½" x 32½" light print border strips to the top and bottom. Press all seam allowances toward the borders.

2. Position, pin, and sew the 1" x 32½" green print strips to the sides of the quilt. Then add the 1" x 33½" green print strips to the top and bottom of the quilt. Press the seam allowances toward the green fabric.

3. In the same manner, add the 4½" x 33½" light print border strips to the sides of the quilt. Then add the 4½" x 41½" light print border strips to the top and bottom of the quilt. Press the seam allowances toward the outer borders.

4. To add the border appliqués, first position the corner leaf and blueberry clusters (a). Then place the center clusters on all 4 sides (b). Finally, position the remaining 8 clusters until you are satisfied with the balance. I placed mine approximately 8" from the center clusters (c).

5. After fusing the appliqués in place, stitch around their edges using the same stitch and thread you selected for the block appliqués.

Finishing

Refer to "Quilting" on page 11 and "Binding Your Quilt" on page 12 for more detailed instructions on finishing techniques, if needed.

1. Piece or trim the quilt backing so that it is 4" larger than the quilt top.

2. Layer the quilt top with batting and backing, and baste the layers together.

3. Quilt and bind using your favorite method.

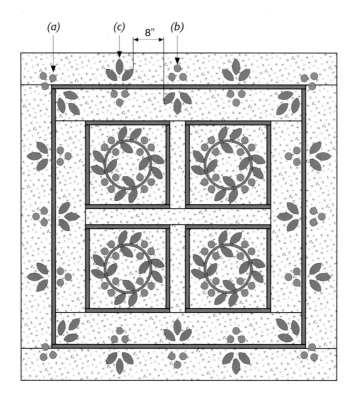

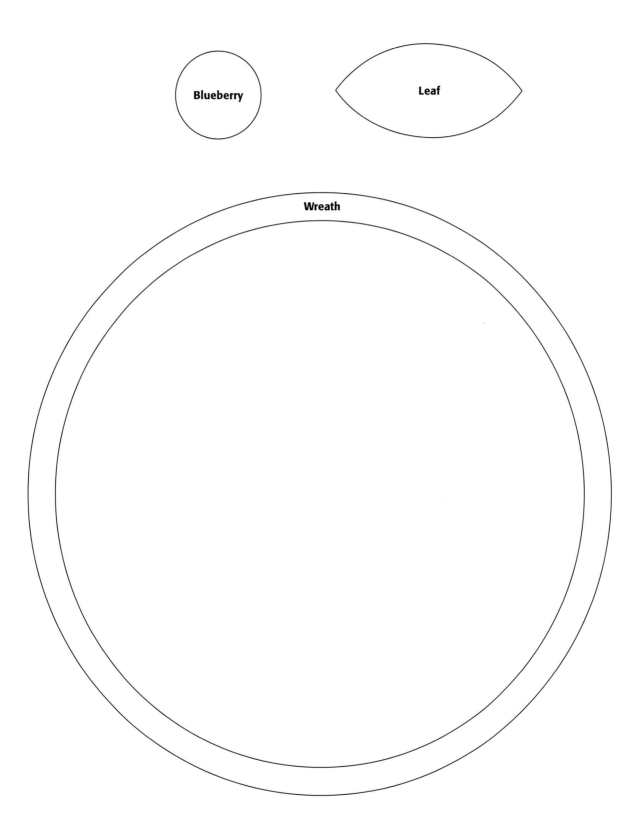

Cherry Baskets

Finished quilt size: 54½" x 54¾"
Finished block size: 8" x 8"

Materials

Yardage is based on 42"-wide fabric unless otherwise stated.

2¼ yds. light floral print for blocks and borders

12 fat eighths (1½ yds. total) of assorted deep pink small-scale checks and prints for baskets and cherries

1 yd. green print for setting triangles

1 yd. deep pink print for sashing, border, and binding

Scraps of green prints for leaves

3⅜ yds. fabric for backing

59" x 59" piece of batting

1 yd. fusible web (17" wide)

Cutting

Patterns for the basket, cherry, and leaf are on page 68.

From each of the fat eighths, cut:
1 basket (12 total)
1 cherry (12 total; cherries may match baskets or not)

From the green scraps, cut:
1 pair of leaves for each basket (24 total)

From the light floral print, cut:
12 squares, 8½" x 8½"
2 strips, 4½" x 47", on the lengthwise grain
2 strips, 5" x 55", on the lengthwise grain
2 strips, 5" x 46", on the lengthwise grain

From the green yardage, cut:
5 squares, 13" x 13"; cut in half diagonally twice to yield 20 side setting triangles
6 squares, 7" x 7"; cut in half diagonally once to yield 12 corner triangles

From the deep pink print, cut:
10 strips, 1" x 42"
6 strips, 2½" x 42"

Strippy-style quilts are a fun way to showcase a large-scale print. You don't have to slice them up into tiny bits and lose the beauty of their design. In this quilt, I used a floral print on a light background in both the wide stripes and the border, as well as in the backgrounds of the cherry baskets. The light print is a nice foil for the bold red baskets and green setting triangles.

Making the Blocks

1. Referring to "Using Fusible Web" on page 8, prepare the baskets, cherries, and leaves for appliqué. To reduce stiffness, cut out the centers of the fusible web on the basket pieces.

2. Position each basket, its cherry, and leaves on point on an 8½" x 8½" light floral print block. After fusing the shapes in place, sew around all appliqués using a machine blanket stitch.

Placement Diagram

Assembling the Quilt Top

1. Assemble 4 Basket blocks and 6 green side setting triangles (cut from the 13" squares) into a vertical row, stitching units together as shown. The triangles are slightly oversized and will be trimmed later.

2. Sew the corner triangles (cut from the 7" squares) on last. Repeat until you have 3 rows.

Make 3.

3. Using a rotary cutter and a ruler, trim the excess triangle fabric, leaving a ¼" seam allowance all the way around the pieced strips. Cut the long sides first, then the short sides, squaring off the corners.

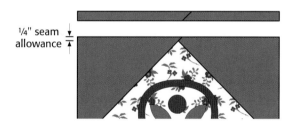

¼" seam allowance

4. Measure the length of all 3 completed vertical rows. They should measure approximately 45¾". If they differ, estimate the average and consider this the length. Sew 7 of the deep pink 1" x 42" strips together end to end. From this long strip, cut 6 sashing strips to 45¾" (or your average length).

5. Sew a deep pink sashing strip to each long side of all 3 basket rows.

6. Trim the 2 light floral print 4½" x 47" sashing strips to the same length as your basket rows. Sew the basket rows and floral rows together as shown.

7. Measure the width of the quilt through the center. It should measure approximately 45½". Sew the remaining 3 deep pink 1" x 42" strips together end to end. From this long strip, cut 2 pieces equal to the width of your quilt top. Sew the strips to the top and bottom of the quilt.

8. Trim 2 of the 5"-wide floral print border strips to the length of the quilt top (approximately 45¾"). Sew them to the sides of the quilt.

9. Trim the remaining 2 floral print 5" border strips to the width of the quilt top (approximately 54½"). Sew them to the top and bottom of the quilt.

Finishing

Refer to "Quilting" on page 11 and "Binding Your Quilt" on page 12 for more detailed instructions on finishing techniques, if needed.

1. Piece the quilt backing so it is 4" larger than the quilt top.
2. Layer the quilt top with batting and backing, and baste the layers together.
3. Quilt and bind using your favorite method.

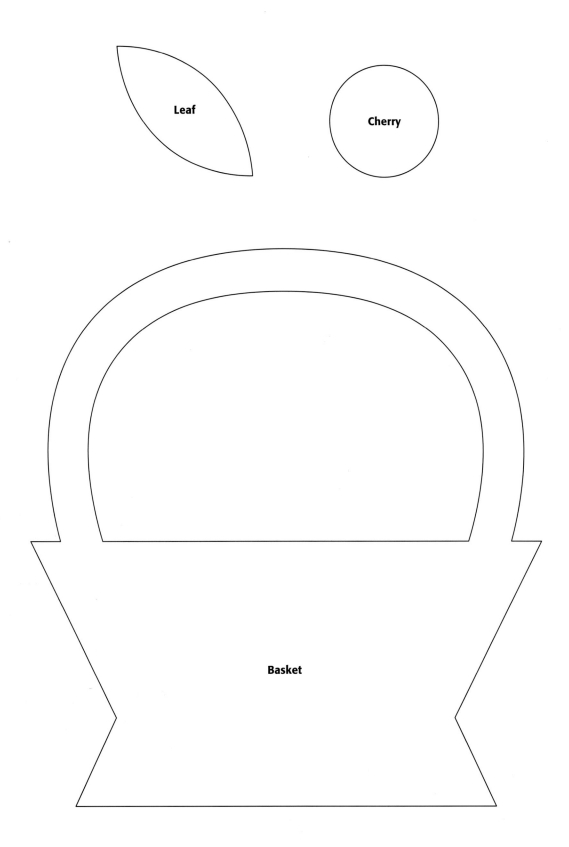

Blueberry Pie

Finished quilt size: 33½" x 33½"
Finished block size: 9" x 9"

Materials

Yardage is based on 42"-wide fabric.

1¼ yds. blue print for blocks, border, and binding

1 yd. light print for blocks and border

¼ yd. yellow print for blocks

1⅛ yds. fabric for backing

38" x 38" piece of batting

Cutting

From the blue print, cut:
8 strips, 1½" x 27½"
3 strips, 1½" x 42"
6 strips, 2" x 42"; crosscut into 108 squares, 2" x 2"
4 strips, 2½" x 42"

From the light print, cut:
4 strips, 1½" x 27½"
3 strips, 1½" x 42"
2 strips, 2" x 42"; crosscut into 36 squares, 2" x 2"
6 strips, 2" x 42"; crosscut into 36 rectangles, 2" x 6½"

From the yellow print, cut:
2 strips, 3½" x 42"; crosscut into 36 rectangles, 2" x 3½"

Making the Nine-Patch Units

1. Gather the 3 blue and 3 light 1½" x 42" strips. (Set aside the 27½" strips for now.) Make 2 strip sets, one alternating light/blue/light and the other alternating blue/light/blue. Press all seam allowances toward the blue strips.

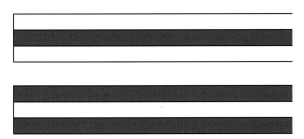

Make 1 each.

This easy, cheerful quilt brings to mind fresh blueberries and summer sunshine.

2. Crosscut the strip sets into 1½" segments. You need 17 light/blue/light segments and 22 blue/light/blue segments.

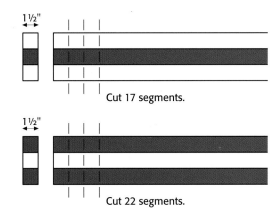

1½"

Cut 17 segments.

1½"

Cut 22 segments.

3. Sew the segments together to make a total of 13 nine-patch units. You need 9 units with blue corners, sewn as shown. Piece 4 units with light corners, as shown. Set aside these 4 units for the border.

Make 9. Make 4.

Piecing the Blocks

1. To both sides of a nine-patch unit with blue corners, add a 2" x 3½" yellow rectangle. Repeat for all 9 units.

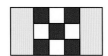

Make 9.

2. Sew a 2" blue square to both ends of the remaining 18 yellow 2" x 3½" rectangles.

Make 18.

3. Add a blue-and-yellow unit to the top and bottom of all 9 blocks.

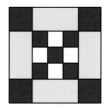

Make 9.

4. Place a 2" blue square on each end of a 2" x 6½" light rectangle, right sides together, raw edges even. Sew across the diagonals, as shown.

5. Trim off the outer corners, leaving a ¼" seam allowance. Press the remaining triangles back. You need 36 of these units.

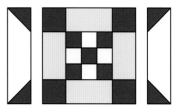

Make 36.

6. Sew units made in step 5 to opposite sides of a block, as shown. You'll use 18 units for the 9 blocks.

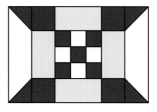

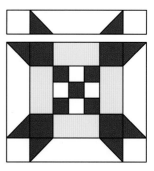

Make 9.

7. Sew a 2" light square to each end of the remaining 18 units. Sew these to the top and bottom of the 9 blocks to complete them.

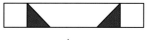

Make 18.

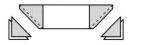

Make 9.

70

Assembling the Quilt Top

1. Arrange the blocks in 3 rows of 3 blocks each. Sew the blocks together in horizontal rows. Press the seams to one side, then sew the rows together.

2. Create 4 striped borders by stitching the 1½" x 27½" blue strips and light strips into blue/light/blue strip sets, as shown.

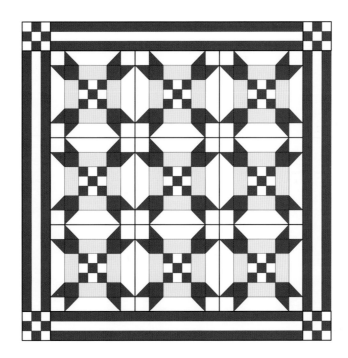

Make 4.

3. Sew a striped border to the left and right sides of the quilt top.

4. Sew a nine-patch unit with light corners onto each end of the 2 remaining striped borders. Sew these borders to the top and bottom of the quilt.

Finishing

Refer to "Quilting" on page 11 and "Binding Your Quilt" on page 12 for more detailed instructions on finishing techniques, if needed.

1. Trim the quilt backing so that it is 4" larger than the quilt top.

2. Layer the quilt top with batting and backing, and baste the layers together.

3. Quilt and bind using your favorite method.

Strawberries and Cream

Finished quilt size: 41½" x 41½"
Finished block size: 9" x 9"

Materials

Yardage is based on 42"-wide fabric unless otherwise stated.

1¼ yds. muslin for blocks and borders

1¼ yds. green for stems, scallops, sashing squares, and binding

⅝ yd. floral print for sashing and borders

⅜ yd. dark pink or red print for strawberries

⅛ yd. light pink solid for buds

⅛ yd. or scraps of gold for flower centers

2⅝ yds. fabric for backing

46" x 46" piece of batting

2 yds. fusible web (17" wide)

Water-soluble fabric marker

Cutting

Patterns for the strawberry, bud, stem, center, and corner and side scallops are on page 76.

From the dark pink or red print, cut:
32 strawberries

From the light pink solid, cut:
32 buds

From the green, cut:
32 stems
9 squares, 2½" x 2½"
4 corner scallops
12 side scallops
5 strips, 2½" x 42"

From the gold, cut:
4 flower centers

I grew up in Ventura County, California, the strawberry capital of the world. The arrival of spring was marked by the strawberry stands that appeared at the sides of the roads. We'd eat berries until our hands were stained red. Strawberry pie, strawberry jam, strawberry shortcake ... I loved them all, but my favorite was (and remains) strawberries and cream.

From the muslin, cut:
4 squares, 9½" x 9½"
2 strips, 7" x 24½"
2 strips, 7" x 37½"

From the floral print, cut:
12 pieces, 2½" x 9½"
2 strips, 2½" x 37½"
2 strips, 2½" x 41½"

Making the Blocks

1. Referring to "Using Fusible Web" on page 8, prepare the strawberries, buds, stems, centers, and corner and side scallops for appliqué. On all strawberries, cut out the centers of the fusible web. (Put the scallops and 16 of the strawberries, with buds and stems, aside for later.)

2. To help you position the appliqué pieces, draw an X across each 9½" muslin square with the water-soluble fabric marker.

3. Refer to the placement diagram below. Fuse the appliqués onto each block. The 4 strawberry points should meet at the center mark. Place the stems under the strawberries and the buds under the stems. The flower center covers the strawberry points. Use a machine blanket stitch and neutral thread to stitch around the edges of all appliqué pieces. Complete 4 blocks.

Placement Diagram

Assembling the Quilt Top

1. Sew a 2½" green square to a 2½" x 9½" rectangle of floral print; add a second green square, another floral rectangle, and a third green square to complete 1 sashing row. Repeat to make a total of 3 horizontal sashing rows.

2. To make the block rows, sew a 2½" x 9½" floral print strip to opposite sides of an appliqué block. Then join another block and a final floral print strip to this second block. Repeat, joining the other 2 blocks and the floral print strips to make a total of 2 block rows.

3. Sew the block rows and sashing rows together as shown to complete the quilt center.

Adding and Appliquéing the Borders

1. Sew the 7" x 24½" muslin border strips to the sides of the quilt. Then sew the 7" x 37½" muslin border strips to the top and bottom of the quilt.

2. Sew the 2½" x 37½" floral print border strips to the sides of the quilt. Then sew the 2½" x 41½" floral print border strips to the top and bottom of the quilt.

3. Use the water-soluble fabric marker to mark placement lines to position scallops on the borders. Mark a line around the muslin border, 3" from the seam line where the muslin is joined to the outer floral border (a). Use a ruler to mark a diagonal line at each corner from the outside border to the interior sash corners (b).

Measure and mark the exact center of all 4 sides of the quilt (c).

4. Pin the green scallops in place one at a time. Pin a center side scallop first; position it with its ends touching the placement line and its

center lining up with the centerline. (About ½" of muslin shows below the scallop.) Next, position the scallops on either side. After all side scallops are placed, pin the 4 corner scallops. Press each scallop in place, removing the pins first.

5. Position, pin, and press the border strawberries, stems, and buds in place. The diagonal guidelines will help you position the corner appliqués.

6. Sew around all appliqué edges using a machine blanket stitch and neutral thread.

Finishing

Refer to "Quilting" on page 11 and "Binding Your Quilt" on page 12 for more detailed instructions on finishing techniques, if needed.

1. Piece the quilt backing so it is 4" larger than the quilt top.

2. Layer the quilt top with batting and backing, and baste the layers together.

3. Quilt and bind using your favorite method.

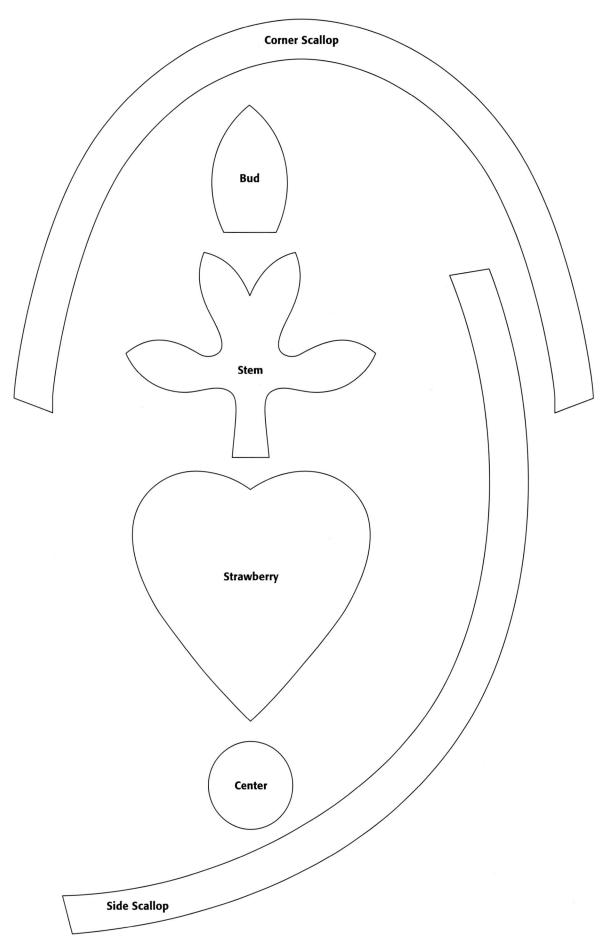

Cherry Four Patch

I'm always drawn to vintage kitchen fabrics from the 1920s and 1930s. This little quilt is an attempt to imitate the cheerful colors—tomato red, lime green, and golden yellow—so often combined in those wonderful old linens. Use this project to decorate your vintage-look kitchen, or any wall that's in need of some brightening up!

Finished quilt size: 31½" x 31½"
Finished block size: 5" x 5"

Materials

Yardage is based on 42"-wide fabric unless otherwise stated.

½ yd. light green print for inner border and binding

⅜ yd. beige check for block backgrounds

⅜ yd. red check for outer border

⅛ yd. brown print for stems

⅛ yd. *each* or scraps of assorted red, green, and yellow prints and solids for cherries and patchwork

1 yd. fabric for backing

36" x 36" piece of batting

¾ yd. fusible web (17" wide)

Cutting

Patterns for the cherry, stem, and leaf are on page 79.

From the assorted reds, cut:
26 cherries
16 squares, 3" x 3"

From the brown print, cut:
13 stems

From the assorted greens, cut:
13 leaves
16 squares, 3" x 3"

From the beige check, cut:
13 squares, 5½" x 5½"

From the assorted yellows, cut:
16 squares, 3" x 3"

From the light green print, cut:
2 strips, 1" x 25½"
2 strips, 1" x 26½"
4 strips, 2½" x 42"

From the red check, cut:
2 strips, 3" x 26½"
2 strips, 3" x 31½"

Making the Appliquéd Blocks

1. Referring to "Using Fusible Web" on page 8, prepare the cherries, stems, and leaves for appliqué.
2. Arrange a cherry cluster (1 stem, 2 cherries, 1 leaf) on each 5½" beige check square.

3. Stitch around the edges of all appliqué pieces, using a machine blanket stitch and black thread to complete 13 Cherry blocks.

Piecing the Four Patch Blocks

Use the assembly-line method (see page 7) to sew 12 Four Patch blocks from the 3" red, green, and yellow squares. Use 2 red squares and 2 yellow or green squares per block, and position the squares so the red ones are in opposite corners. Work in as many cheerful color variations as you can.

Assembling the Quilt Top

1. Referring to the assembly diagram below, lay out the Four Patch and Cherry blocks in 5 rows of 5 blocks each. Experiment with different arrangements to achieve color balance and the best distribution of lights and darks.

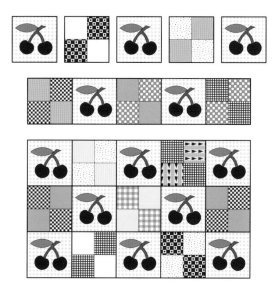

2. Sew the blocks together in horizontal rows, then join the rows together.
3. Measure your quilt; it should be 25½" x 25½". (If not, see "Adding Borders" on page 10.) To

make the inner border, pin and sew 1" x 25½" light green print strips to the left and right sides of the quilt top. Sew the 1" x 26½" strips to the top and bottom of the quilt.

4. To make the outer border, add the 3" x 26½" red check border strips to the sides of the quilt. Then sew the 3" x 31½" strips to the top and bottom of the quilt.

Finishing

Refer to "Quilting" on page 11 and "Binding Your Quilt" on page 12 for more detailed instructions on finishing techniques, if needed.

1. Trim the quilt backing so it is 4" larger than the quilt top.
2. Layer the quilt top with batting and backing, and baste the layers together.
3. Quilt and bind using your favorite method.

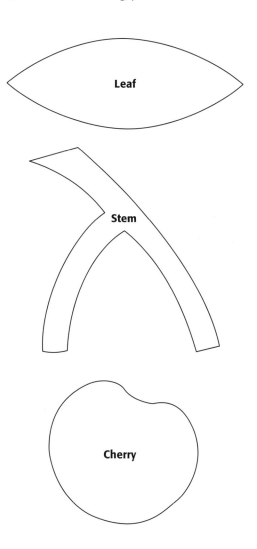

Poinsettia Wreaths

Finished quilt size: 59½" x 59½"
Finished block size: 13" x 13"

Materials

Yardage is based on 42"-wide fabric unless otherwise stated.

⅓ yd. *each* of 4 different light prints for 3½" borders

¼ yd. *each* of 2 different light prints for 2½" vertical sashes

¼ yd. *each* of 8 *or more* different light prints for blocks (the more fabrics, the "scrappier" the look)

⅛ yd. *each* of 3 different light prints for horizontal sashes

1 yd. green print for outer border

1 yd. *total* of scraps of assorted pink and light and dark red prints, checks, and plaids for poinsettia petals

½ yd. *total* of scraps of assorted green prints, checks, and plaids for leaves

⅜ yd. *total* of scraps of assorted golds for poinsettia centers and leaves

4 yds. fabric for backing

⅝ yd. fabric for binding

63" x 63" piece of batting

4 yds. fusible web

Water-soluble fabric marker

Cutting

Patterns for the poinsettia petals (A–E), leaves (F–I), and poinsettia center (J) are on page 84.

From the assorted pink and red scraps, cut:
36 each of patterns A–E

From the assorted green scraps, cut:
36 each of patterns F–H

Like many of the other quilts in this book, much of the charm of this Christmas quilt comes from its varied mix of fabrics. Rather than buy one big piece of beige fabric, use more than a dozen different ivory and beige prints: you'll have a much more interesting background. And select many reds, pinks, and greens for the poinsettias—just as Mother Nature does!

From the gold scraps, cut:
64 of pattern I
108 of pattern J

From the 8 or more different ¼ yd. light prints, cut:
36 squares, 7" x 7"

From the 4 different ⅓ yd. light prints, cut:
6 strips, 3½" x 42"

From the 3 different ⅛ yd. light prints, cut:
3 strips, 2½" x 42"

From the 2 different ¼ yd. light prints, cut:
6 strips, 2½" x 13½"

From the green print, cut:
6 strips, 5½" x 42"

From the binding fabric, cut:
7 strips, 2½" x 42"

Making the Blocks

1. Referring to "Using Fusible Web" on page 8, prepare the poinsettia petals, leaves, and poinsettia centers for appliqué. Label each piece with the pattern letter. Because there are so many similarly shaped pieces for these blocks, do not remove the web paper until you're ready to position each piece.

Placement Diagram

Perfect Placement

Precise placement of each appliqué piece is important in creating the wreath effect in this quilt. I suggest you mark placement lines on each background block using a water-soluble fabric marker to guide you. Divide the block in half vertically, horizontally, and diagonally in both directions. Then refer to the placement diagram to position your appliqué pieces correctly.

2. Arrange poinsettia petals and leaves A–H, then 3 poinsettia centers, on each 7" light print square. When you have the most pleasing color coordination on all 36 blocks, remove the paper backing on the appliqués and reposition them. Do this one block at a time! Fuse the pieces in place, then use a machine blanket stitch and matching thread to stitch around all appliqué edges.

3. Arrange 4 Poinsettia blocks together, turning each successive block 90° to create the wreath design. (*Note:* The corner of each block that points toward the center of the 4-block unit is marked on the placement diagram.) The dark green leaf G should always be on the outside corner. Sew the 4 blocks together to create a 13½" x 13½" Wreath block. You need 9 Wreath blocks.

Make 9.

Assembling the Quilt Top

1. Join the blocks with the 2½" x 13½" light print sashing strips. Sew 3 Wreath blocks and 2 sashing strips together side by side to make one row. Repeat to make 3 rows.

Make 3.

2. Measure the 3-block rows. They should measure 43½" long. If they are different lengths, take the average length. Sew 2 *identical* 2½" light strips together. From the long strip, cut one sashing strip the same length as your block row. Repeat to make a second sashing strip from a different light fabric.

3. Sew the block rows and long sashing strips together as shown.

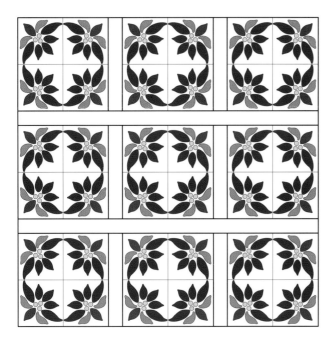

Adding the Borders

1. The 4 light print inner border strips are pieced to fit. Use 4 different fabrics, one for each border. Piece 2 borders 3½" x 43½" (or the length of your quilt) and sew them to the left and right sides of the quilt top. Piece 2 more strips, 3½" x 49½" (or the width of your quilt) and sew them to the top and bottom of the quilt top.
2. Appliqué 4 gold leaves at each intersection of light print border and sashes.

3. Sew 3 green print 5½" x 42" border strips together end to end; repeat to make 2 such long strips. Measure the length of the quilt through the center. It should be approximately 49½" long. From one of the long border strips, cut 2 borders, 5½" x 49½" (or the length of your quilt). Sew them to the left and right sides of the quilt top. Then measure again and cut 2 more borders from the remaining long strip. These should be 59½" long (or the length of your quilt). Sew them to the top and bottom of your quilt.

Finishing

Refer to "Quilting" on page 11 and "Binding Your Quilt" on page 12 for more detailed instructions on finishing techniques, if needed.

1. Piece the quilt backing so it is 4" larger than the quilt top.
2. Layer the quilt top with batting and backing, and baste the layers together.
3. Quilt and bind using your favorite method.

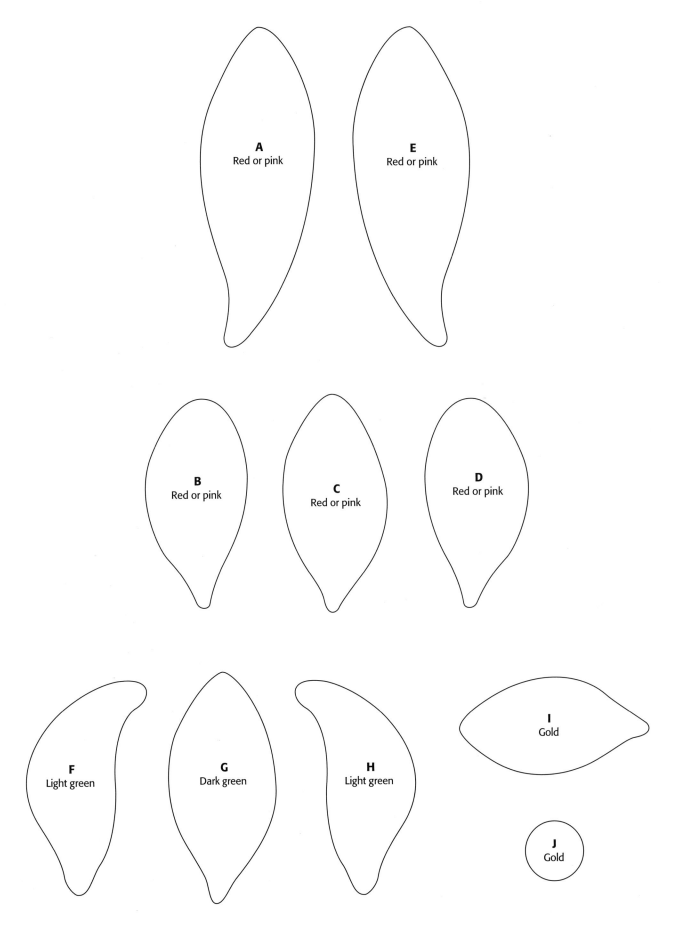

Christmas Posies

Capture the spirit of Christmases past with the homespun feel of this lap-size quilt. The woven plaids are soft and cozy, which is sure to make this quilt a favorite to snuggle under while waiting for Santa to arrive. The lack of a border on this quilt adds to its old-fashioned flavor.

Finished quilt size: 54½" x 54½"
Finished block size: 6" x 6"

Materials

Yardage is based on 42"-wide fabric unless otherwise stated.

1¾ yds. beige check or print for appliquéd blocks and pieced blocks

1½ yds. brown check or print for appliquéd and pieced blocks

1¼ yds. green print for pieced blocks and binding

⅛ yd. brown solid for stems

⅜ yd. *total* of scraps of assorted reds for posies

⅜ yd. *total* of scraps of assorted greens for leaves

Scrap of yellow for posy centers

3½ yds. fabric for backing

59" x 59" piece of batting

1¾ yd. fusible web (17" wide)

Water-soluble fabric marker

Cutting

Patterns for the posy, posy center, bud, stems, and leaf are on page 89.

From the red scraps, cut:
25 posies
100 buds

From the yellow scrap, cut:
25 posy centers

From the brown solid, cut:
100 stems (10 groups of 10)

From the green scraps, cut:
200 leaves

From the brown check or print, cut:
16 squares, 6½" x 6½"
6 strips, 1½" x 42"
10 strips 1½" x 42"; crosscut into 80 rectangles,
     1½" x 4½"

From the green print, cut:
3 strips, 2½" x 42"
12 strips, 1½" x 42"

From the beige check or print, cut:
25 squares, 6½" x 6½"
3 strips, 2½" x 42"
3 strips, 4½" x 42"

Piecing the Blocks

This quilt contains 40 pieced blocks. The directions are for quick-and-easy assembly-line piecing. You won't even have to cut the threads until the last seam has been sewn.

1. Sew a 1½" x 42" brown check strip to each side of a 2½" x 42" green print strip. Repeat to make 3 identical strip sets. Crosscut the 3 strip sets into 2½" rectangles, to yield 40 units.

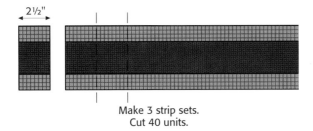

2½"

Make 3 strip sets.
Cut 40 units.

2. Sew a 1½" x 42" green strip to each side of a 2½" x 42" beige check strip. Repeat to make 3 identical strip sets. Crosscut the 3 strip sets into 1½" units, as shown. You need 80 units.

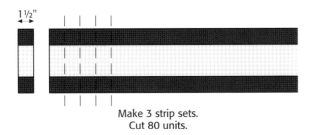

1½"

Make 3 strip sets.
Cut 80 units.

3. Sew a 1½" x 42" green strip to each side of a 4½" x 42" beige check strip. Repeat to make 3 identical strip sets. Crosscut the 3 strip sets into 1½" units, as shown. You need 80 units.

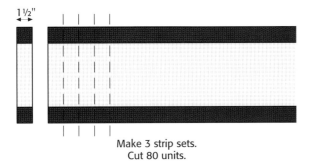

1½"

Make 3 strip sets.
Cut 80 units.

4. Piece 40 blocks as shown. The fastest way is to sew all 40 units without cutting the thread. Then add the next rectangle to all 40 units, continuing in this fashion until all blocks are pieced.

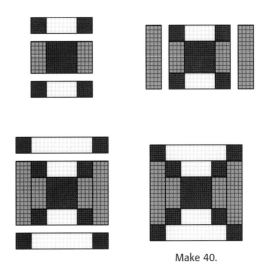

Make 40.

Making the Appliquéd Blocks

1. Referring to "Using Fusible Web" on page 8, prepare the posies, posy centers, buds, stems, and leaves for appliqué.

Preparing for Scrap Appliqué

Trace all your template shapes onto the wrong side of fusible web at one time. Then iron the web to the wrong side of many assorted fabric scraps to really mix things up. Cut out the shapes, but don't peel the paper off. Put the appliqué pieces into separate containers or zip-top plastic bags—one for posies, one for leaves, and so forth. That way, you'll have lots of colors to choose from as you prepare each block, and your finished quilt will be quite scrappy and fun.

2. Assemble 9 beige check 6½" squares and 16 brown check 6½" squares. (Set aside the remaining 16 beige squares until later.) These are your 25 appliqué blocks. Using the water-soluble marker, mark an X through the diagonal center of each block to help position the appliqués.

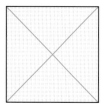 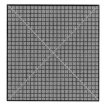

3. Refer to the placement diagram below. Position a posy on each of the 9 beige squares and 16 brown squares. Next, place 4 stems under the center posy and add the buds and leaves using a variety of reds and greens in each block. Remove the paper backing and fuse the appliqués in place as you go. Using a ⅛" blanket stitch and matching thread, stitch around all appliqué edges.

Placement Diagram

Assembling the Quilt Top

1. Lay out the 81 blocks on your floor or a design wall (25 appliquéd blocks, 40 pieced blocks, and 16 plain blocks). Alternate the appliquéd blocks with the pieced blocks, and place the 16 plain beige check blocks around the outside edges of the quilt.

2. The pieced blocks have 2 light sides and 2 dark sides. The light beige appliquéd blocks must always adjoin the light sides of the pieced blocks around them. The brown appliquéd blocks must always adjoin the dark sides of the pieced blocks around them.

   Change the orientation of the pieced blocks 90° (a quarter-turn) to ensure that the correct shades are adjacent. Move appliquéd blocks as needed until bright and dark reds are in balance. Number the blocks to keep them in order. Sew row by row.

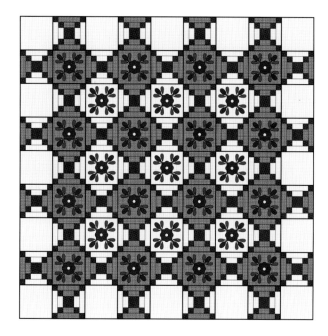

Finishing

Refer to "Quilting" on page 11 and "Binding Your Quilt" on page 12 for more detailed instructions on finishing techniques, if needed.

1. Piece the quilt backing so it is 4" larger than the quilt top.
2. Layer the quilt top with batting and backing, and baste the layers together.
3. Quilt and bind using your favorite method.

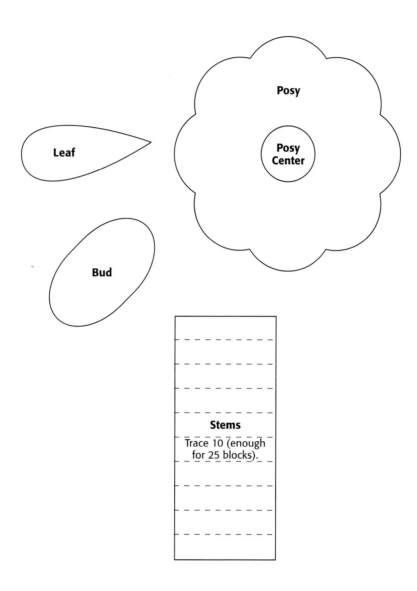

Leaf

Posy

Posy Center

Bud

Stems
Trace 10 (enough
for 25 blocks).

Snowmen Tree Skirt

Finished size: 40" diameter

Materials

Yardage is based on 42"-wide fabric unless otherwise stated.

¼ yd. *each* of 7 different green prints and solids for trees

1¼ yds. red for background

⅜ yd. tea-dyed muslin for snowmen

⅛ yd. black solid for hats and broomsticks

⅛ yd. *total* of scraps of gold for stars and broom straws

Colorful scraps for scarves, mittens, buttons, hatbands, cheeks, noses, and broomstick bindings

1⅓ yds. fabric for backing★

½ yd. fabric for binding

45" x 45" piece of batting

2¼ yds. heavy-duty fusible web

24" length of string or crochet thread

Black permanent marker

★ *If the fabric is not at least 42" wide, you will need to piece the backing, which requires 2½ yards of fabric.*

Cutting

Patterns for the snowman pieces, star, and tree are on pages 94–95. See step 1 in "Preparing the Skirt" for cutting the skirt and its backing.

From the tea-dyed muslin, cut:
8 snowmen

From the black solid, cut:
8 hats
8 broomsticks

From the colorful scraps, cut:
8 scarves
8 mittens
16 buttons
8 broomstick bindings

Whimsical snowmen wearing quite stylish hats stand erect between tall evergreen trees all around this Christmas-red quilted tree skirt. Fusible web makes the appliqué easy—I didn't even bother to stitch the appliqué edges in place. I figured this was one project that wouldn't get a lot of wear and tear.

From the green prints and solids, cut:
1 tree from each fabric (7 total)

From the gold scraps, cut:
8 stars
8 broom straws

Preparing the Skirt

1. Open the red fabric and press it smooth. Spread it out on a table or the floor and mark the exact center with the black permanent marker. (Don't worry: it will be cut out later.) Tie the string or crochet thread around a pencil or the black marker (the marker is easier to see against the red fabric and will be trimmed off). Cut the string so it is exactly 20" long. With one hand, hold the loose end of the string on the center mark, and with the other hand draw a 40" circle around the fabric with the pen vertical. Cut out the circle just inside the drawn line.

2. Turn the fabric over, wrong side up. Divide the circle into 8 wedges by folding the circle in half (right side is now up), then folding it in half again, then folding it in half again, to create 8 layers.

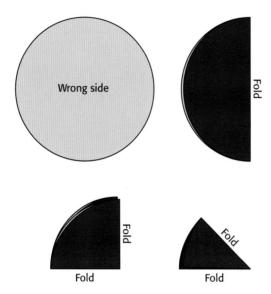

3. Clip ⅛" at the circle edge wherever there is a fold. Or mark the fold lines with pins at the circle edge. Unfold the fabric and use a ruler and pencil (not a pen, which might bleed through) to draw straight lines from the center dot to the clipped edges on the wrong side of the fabric.

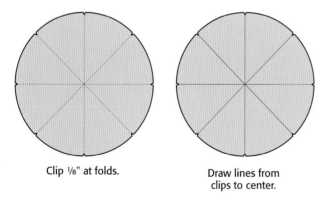

Clip ⅛" at folds.   Draw lines from clips to center.

4. Use a large needle and white thread to hand baste along the drawn pencil lines. Stitches can be as long as 2"; they will be removed later. The right side of your red fabric now has white basting stitches to help you place the appliqués.

5. You need a center hole to accommodate your Christmas tree trunk. On the right side of the fabric, use a pencil and a bowl or small plate to draw a circle in the center. (My circle is approximately 6¼" in diameter.) Cut out the circle.

Appliquéing the Motifs

1. Referring to "Using Fusible Web" on page 8, prepare 8 snowmen (and all associated pieces), 8 stars, and 7 trees for appliqué. If you do not plan to stitch around the edges of the appliqué, I recommend using heavy-duty fusible web. It has a stronger hold than the lightweight fusible web, but you can't sew through it.

2. Place the 8 snowmen between the white basting lines, approximately 2" away from the outer edge of the circle. Draw their eyes with a permanent black marker, such as an extra fine Sharpie. Add the accessories and brooms and press to fuse them in place.

3. Center the 7 trees over the white basting stitches, approximately 1½" from the outer edge of the circle. *Note:* There are only 7 trees, leaving one white basting line free; it will be cut later as an opening.

4. Fuse the 8 stars in place so their side points are the same height as the tops of the trees. You want them placed as accurately as possible because they create a circle around the inner edge of the tree skirt and you don't want an uneven, wavering circle.

Finishing the Skirt

1. Cut the backing and batting into circles at least 2" larger than the tree skirt all the way around. (Just lay the tree skirt on top of them and "eyeball" this trimming.) If you piece the backing, make a square at least 45" x 45", then trim it into a circle.

2. Layer the backing, batting, and tree skirt; baste with safety pins. The backing and batting will show through the center hole.

3. After the layers are pinned together, cut through all layers along the extra white basting line from the outer edge to the center circle. Place more safety pins along both sides of the cut to make sure the quilt top is securely held.

4. Remove all the basting stitches that can be seen. Leave the stitches that are hidden underneath the trees because trying to get them out may weaken the fusible bond.

5. Quilt by hand or machine. I did a machine outline stitch close to all the appliqué, using a darning foot and free-motion quilting.

6. Trim off excess batting and backing; cut out the center opening.

7. From the binding fabric, cut 2 ties, 1½" x 20". Press under ½" on both short ends, wrong sides together. Press under ¼" along the long edges, wrong sides together. Then fold the ties in half lengthwise and press. Sew along both short ends and the long open end to finish.

8. From the binding fabric, cut 2½"-wide bias strips. You'll need enough strips to go around the outer edge of the tree skirt, along both edges of the cut opening, and the center circle.

9. Apply the binding using your favorite method (or refer to "Binding Your Quilt" on page 12 for more details). Sew ties to the tree skirt at the center circle so it can be tied around the tree trunk.

Star

Snowman

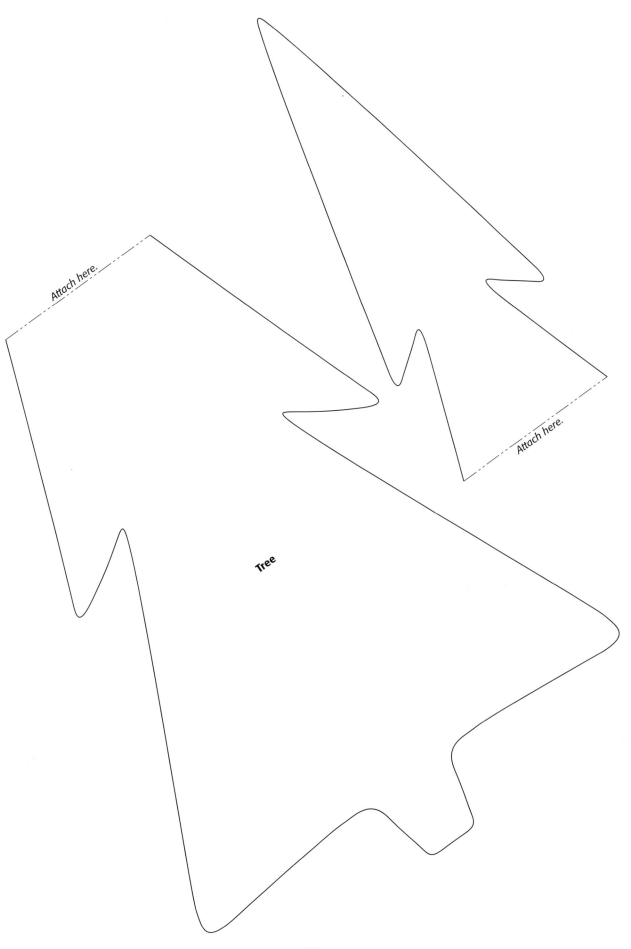

Attach here.

Attach here.

Tree

Little Socks Table Runner

Finished size: 16" x 38"

Materials

Yardage is based on 42"-wide fabric unless otherwise stated.

¼ yd. *each* of 5 colorful prints for socks

½ yd. muslin for background and middle border

¼ yd. green for inner and outer borders

¼ yd. red for letters

⅛ yd. gold for stars

Scraps of assorted colorful prints for sock heels, toes, and top bands

⅝ yd. fabric for backing

20" x 42" piece of batting

1½ yds. fusible web (17" wide)

Black embroidery floss

Cutting

Patterns for the stocking, toe, heel, top band, star, and letters are on page 99.

From the muslin, cut:
1 strip, 8½" x 30½"
2 rectangles, 3½" x 8½"
2 strips, 3½" x 30½"
4 squares, 3½" x 3½"

From the 5 colorful prints, cut:
5 stockings (1 from each)

From the assorted colorful scraps, cut:
5 toes
5 heels
5 top bands

From the gold, cut:
4 stars

From the red, cut:
18 sets of letters

Tiny stockings splashed in brightly colored fabrics are a fun way to add a festive touch to your table. Welcome family and friends—and kids of all ages—to gather round for what's sure to be a jolly time.

From the green, cut:
4 strips, 1" x 3½"
2 strips, 1" x 8½"
4 strips, 1" x 37½"
2 strips, 1" x 16½"

Appliquéing the Block and Borders

1. Referring to "Using Fusible Web" on page 8, prepare the stockings, toes, heels, top bands, stars, and 18 sets of letters for appliqué.

2. Fuse the toes, heels, and top bands on the 5 stockings. (Don't peel the backing paper off the stockings before you do this.) Referring to the photograph, arrange the stockings on the 8½" x 30½" muslin rectangle. Note that 2 stockings face one way and 3 face the other way. Tilt them slightly for a whimsical look. Once you get the stockings positioned in a pleasing manner, pin them in place. Remove the pins and press them into place one at a time.

3. To make the table runner machine washable, stitch around all the appliqué edges to secure them. I wanted the stitching on the heels and toes to really stand out, so I used 6 strands of black embroidery floss and

stitched around them by hand with a ⅜" blanket stitch. I did not want the stitching on the other edges to be as noticeable, so I used a ⅛" machine blanket stitch with black thread.

4. Fuse a gold star onto each of the 3½" muslin corner blocks. Stitch around them using a ⅛" machine blanket stitch with black thread.

5. Fuse 7 "Ho" units on each of the 30½" muslin middle border strips. Fuse 2 "Ho" units on each of the 8½" muslin middle border strips. When placing the letters, allow for ¼" seams around the border edges. Then stitch around all edges using a machine blanket stitch with black thread.

Make 2.

Make 2.

Assembling the Table Runner

1. Scw a 1" x 8½" green inner border strip to each short end of the table runner.

2. Sew an 8½" letter border to each end. Make sure the letters are facing the right direction: the base of the letters should always be along the outside edge.

3. Sew 2 of the 1" x 37½" green inner border strips to the top and bottom.

4. Add a 1" x 3½" green strip to each end of the long letter borders, then add a star appliqué square, as shown.

Make 2.

5. Sew the borders to the central portion of the table runner.

6. Sew the remaining 37½" green border strips to the long edges of the table runner. Then sew the 16½" green border strips to the short edges.

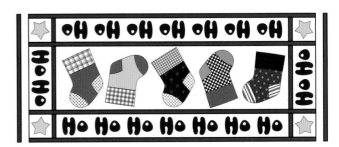

Finishing

Use the quick quilting method (see page 12) rather than binding the table runner.

1. Cut the backing and batting slightly larger than your project. Lay the batting out, and center the backing over it, right side up. Center your quilt top over the first 2 layers, wrong side up.

2. Pin the layers together and sew a ¼" seam around the quilt, leaving an 8" opening.

3. Trim excess backing and batting. Clip the corners, turn the table runner right side out through the opening, press, and stitch the opening.

4. To finish, quilt by hand or machine.

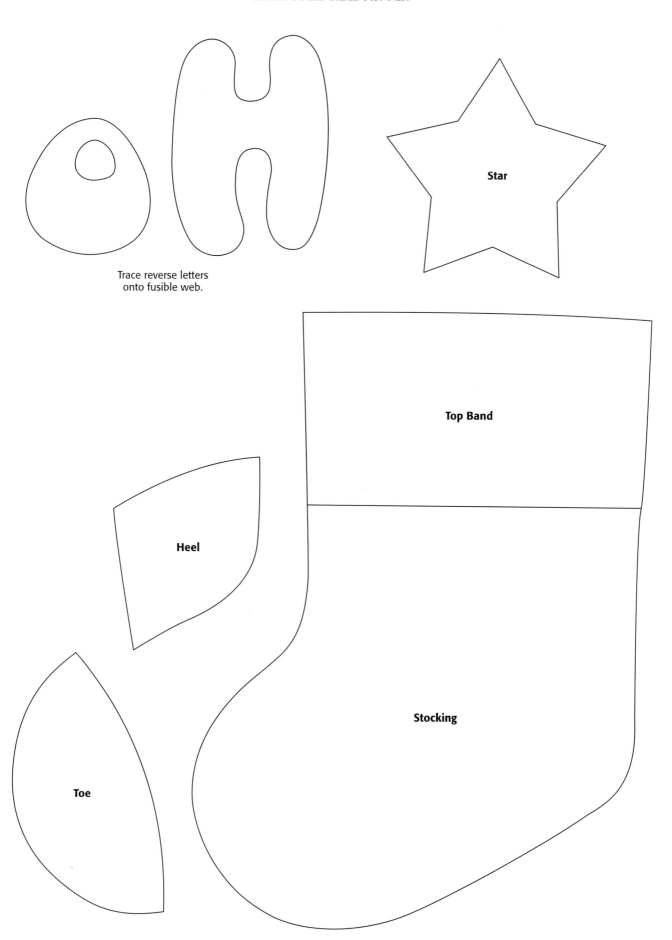

Trace reverse letters
onto fusible web.

Star

Top Band

Heel

Stocking

Toe

Little Stockings

These darling little stockings make great tree or garland decorations, but they're just as much fun to use as party favors to coordinate with the "Little Socks" table runner on page 96. Your guests will love taking their little stockings, filled with candies, small gifts, or simple holiday greenery, home with them.

Finished size: 7" long

Materials

Yardage is based on 42"-wide fabric unless otherwise stated. Materials and directions are for one 7"-long stocking.

¼ yd. or fat quarter for stocking

⅛ yd. contrasting fabric for toe, heel, and band

⅛ yd. fusible web (17" wide)

Template plastic

Black embroidery floss

Cutting

Patterns for the stocking, toe, and heel are on the facing page. See step 1 in "Making a Stocking" for cutting the stocking front and back.

From the contrasting fabric, cut:
2 squares, 5" x 5", for top bands
2 toes
2 heels

Making a Stocking

1. Make a plastic template of the stocking pattern. Trace around the pattern onto a doubled layer of fabric, wrong sides together. Cut out on the line through both layers. This gives you a stocking front and a stocking back.

2. Press both 5" squares in half, wrong sides together, so they measure 2½" x 5".

3. Lay the stocking front and stocking back on your sewing table, right sides up. Place a top band beneath each stocking shape, with top raw edges even. Sew along the top edge, using a ¼" seam.

4. Press the seam allowance toward the band. Fold the band to the front of the stocking so the seam allowance is hidden underneath the band. Trim the sides of the band so the band is even with the stocking.

Fold over stitching.

Trim.

5. Referring to "Using Fusible Web" on page 8, prepare a toe and heel shape and fuse them onto the stocking front (the side that points left when right side up). If you want to appliqué a toe and a heel onto the back as well, trace a reverse toe and heel. Stitch around the appliqué shapes by hand with 6 strands of black embroidery floss and a ⅜" blanket stitch.

6. Place the stocking front and stocking back right sides together. Sew around the outer edge, using a ¼" seam allowance and small stitches. Trim the seam to ¹⁄₁₆" around the curves. Turn right side out and press flat.

7. If you want to hang your stocking, use 6 strands of black embroidery floss to sew a loop to the top.

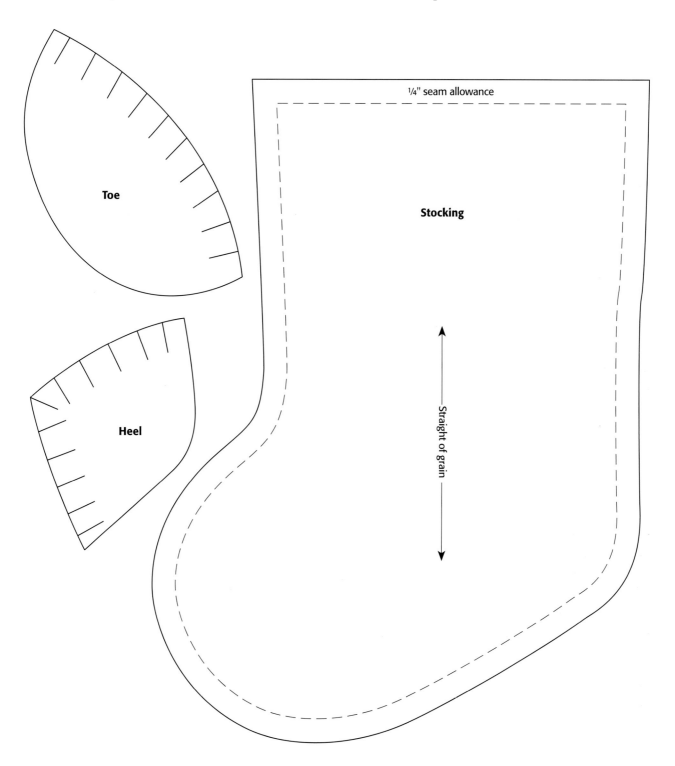

Toe

Heel

Stocking

¼" seam allowance

Straight of grain

Anchors Aweigh

Finished quilt size: 44½" x 44½"
Finished block size: 12" x 12"

Materials

Yardage is based on 42"-wide fabric.

2 yds. nautical border print, if directional (as shown)
OR 1 yd., if nondirectional

1¼ yds. dark blue for wheels, inner border, and binding

¾ yd. off-white solid

½ yd. blue check or gingham for sashing

¼ yd. red for wheel centers and anchors

¼ yd. yellow-gold for stars and squares

2¾ yds. fabric for backing

48" x 48" piece of batting

1½ yds. fusible web (17" wide)

Water-soluble fabric marker

Cutting

*Patterns for the wheel, wheel center, anchor, and star
are on pages 104–105.*

From the dark blue, cut:
4 wheels
2 strips, 1" x 33½"
2 strips, 1" x 34½"
5 strips, 2½" x 42"

From the red, cut:
4 wheel centers
9 anchors

From the yellow-gold, cut:
4 stars
9 squares, 3½" x 3½"

From the off-white solid, cut:
4 squares, 12½" x 12½"

From the blue check or gingham, cut:
12 strips, 3½" x 12½"

*My father used to love visiting the
boat docks near our home in
Southern California. I think it
reminded him of his childhood,
growing up on the beach. He never
did own a boat of his own, but, like
most things, dreaming about it
brought its own kind of joy.*

From the nautical border print, cut:★
2 strips, 5½" x 34½", for top and bottom borders
2 strips, 5½" x 44½", for side borders

★ *If your nautical print is directional, like mine, cut
the top and bottom outer border strips across the
width of the fabric, and the side outer border strips
along the length of the fabric.*

Making the Blocks

1. Referring to "Using Fusible Web" on page
   8, prepare the wheels, wheel centers, stars,
   and anchors for appliqué. Before fusing the
   wheel center pieces to the red fabric, cut
   away excess web out of the centers to
   reduce bulk.

2. Fold the 12½" off-white background blocks
   into quarters and, using the water-soluble
   fabric marker, draw placement lines along
   the fold lines as shown. This will help you
   center the wheels.

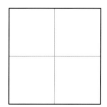

3. Arrange the wheels, wheel centers, and stars on the 4 blocks, and fuse them in place. Stitch around all appliqué edges, using a blanket stitch with matching thread.

Placement Diagram

4. Fuse the red anchors onto the 9 yellow-gold 3½" squares. Stitch the edges with a blanket stitch, using red thread.

Assembling the Quilt Top

1. Sew 3 anchor squares and 2 blue check or gingham sashing strips together, end to end. Repeat to make 3 of these sashing rows.

Make 3.

2. Sew 3 blue check or gingham sashing strips and 2 Wheel blocks together, side by side. Repeat to make a second row.

Make 2.

3. Sew the sashing rows and the Wheel block rows together, beginning with a sashing row and alternating the rows.

4. Sew the 33½" dark blue inner border strips to the left and right sides of the quilt top. Sew the 34½" inner border strips to the top and bottom of the quilt top.

5. Sew the 34½" nautical print outer border strips to the top and bottom of the quilt top. Sew the 44½" outer border strips to the sides of the quilt top.

Finishing

Refer to "Quilting" on page 11 and "Binding Your Quilt" on page 12 for more detailed instructions on finishing techniques, if needed.

1. Piece the quilt backing so it is 4" larger than the quilt top.

2. Layer the quilt top with batting and backing, and baste the layers together.

3. Quilt and bind using your favorite method.

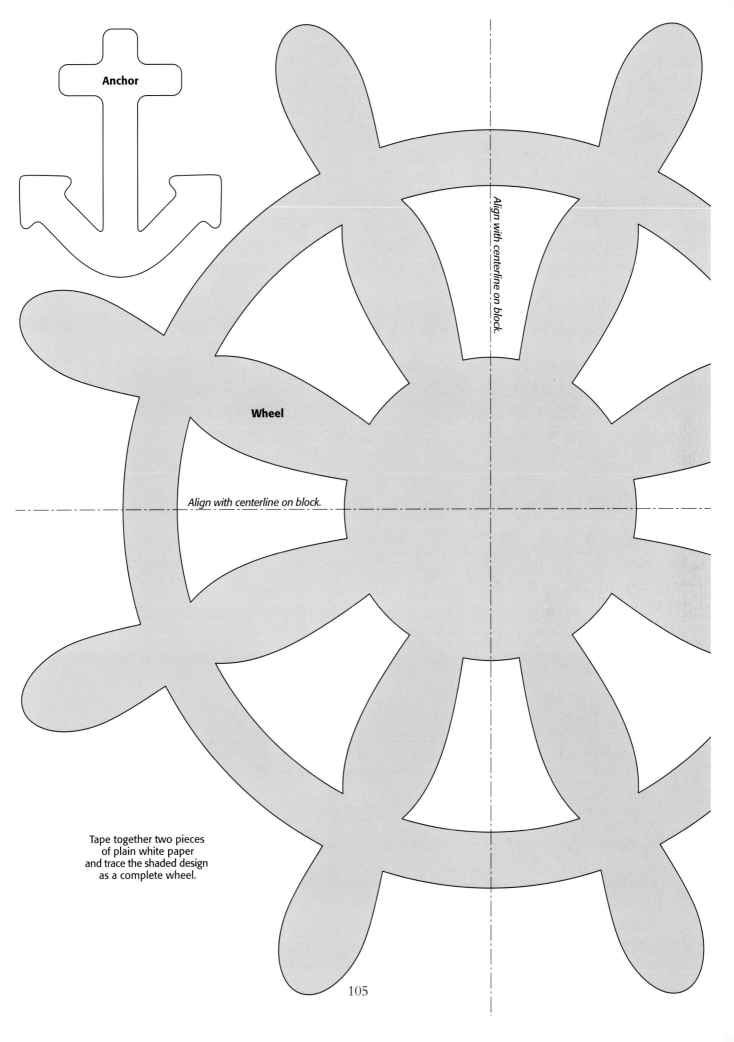

Anchor

Wheel

Align with centerline on block.

Align with centerline on block.

Tape together two pieces
of plain white paper
and trace the shaded design
as a complete wheel.

105

Red Stars

Finished quilt size: 56½" x 72½"
Finished block size: 8" x 8"

Materials

Yardage is based on 42"-wide fabric.

4 yds. muslin for blocks and middle border

2¼ yds. blue for borders and binding

1¾ yds. red for blocks★

3¾ yds. fabric for backing

60" x 76" piece of batting

★ *Red fabrics often bleed. Cut a small swatch and test yours. If it bleeds, pretreat with a solution such as Retayne, or get advice from the staff at your local quilt store.*

Cutting

From the red, cut:

3 strips, 4½" x 42"; crosscut into 18 squares, 4½" x 4½"

9 strips, 2½" x 42"; crosscut into 144 squares, 2½" x 2½"

8 strips, 2" x 42"

2 strips, 2½" x 42"

From the muslin, cut:

5 strips, 4½" x 42"; crosscut into 72 rectangles, 4½" x 2½"

18 strips, 2½" x 42"; crosscut into 296 squares, 2½" x 2½"

4 strips, 2" x 42"

2 strips, 2½" x 42"

4 strips, 3½" x 42"

2 strips, 5½" x 42"

12 strips, 1½" x 42"

From the blue, cut:

4 squares, 4½" x 4½"

8 strips, 4½" x 42"; crosscut into 104 rectangles, 4½" x 2½"

12 strips, 1½" x 42"

7 strips, 2½" x 42"

I love the freshness of red, white, and blue—it never goes out of style. I can't resist including at least one quilt using this color scheme in every book I write. In this quilt, the simplicity of solid red, blue, and off-white muslin is particularly dramatic.

Piecing the Star Blocks

You'll need to make 18 Star blocks for this quilt. The star points are made with 72 flying-geese units.

1. Place a 2½" red square on top of a 2½" x 4½" muslin rectangle, right sides together, raw edges even.

2. Sew across the diagonal, as shown.

3. Cut off the outer corner, leaving a ¼" seam allowance, and press back the remaining red triangle. Repeat on the opposite end of the rectangle to complete a flying-geese unit. Make 72.

Make 72.

4. Use 4 flying-geese units, one 4½" red square, and four 2½" muslin squares to assemble a Star block, as shown. Repeat to make 18 Star blocks.

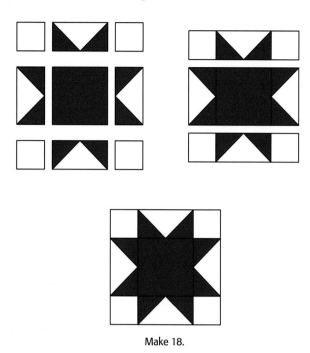

Make 18.

Piecing the Stepping Stone Blocks

1. Sew a 2" red strip to both sides of a 5½" muslin strip. Repeat to make 2 strip sets. Press the seam allowances toward the red strips. Crosscut the strips into 2" units. Cut 34.

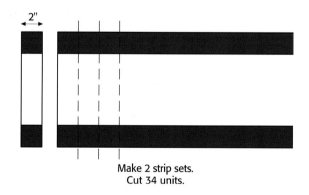

Make 2 strip sets.
Cut 34 units.

2. Sew together 5 strips side by side in the following order: 2" muslin, 2" red, 2½" muslin, 2" red, 2" muslin. Repeat so you have 2 identical strip sets. Press the seam allowances toward the red strips, then crosscut the strip sets into 2" units. Cut 34.

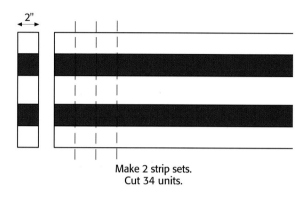

Make 2 strip sets.
Cut 34 units.

3. Sew a 3½" muslin strip to both sides of a 2½" red strip. Make 2 of these strip sets. Press the seam allowances toward the red strips, then crosscut into 2½" units. Cut 17.

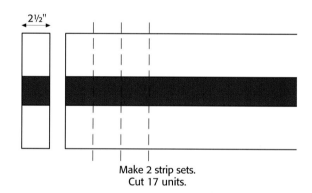

Make 2 strip sets.
Cut 17 units.

4. Assemble the units as shown to make a Stepping Stone block. Repeat to make 17 Stepping Stone blocks.

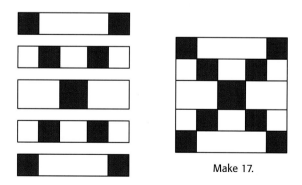

Make 17.

Assembling the Quilt Top

Alternating Star blocks and Stepping Stone blocks, arrange all blocks in rows, 5 across and 7 deep. Sew the blocks together in rows, then sew the rows together.

Adding the Borders

1. To make the inner border, sew 3 of the 1½" blue strips together end to end; from them, cut 2 strips the length of your quilt top (approximately 56½" long). Sew these to the long sides of your quilt top.

2. Measure the length of 2 more 1½" blue strips. If they are at least 42½", you can use them for your top and bottom borders. If they are not long enough, piece together 3 strips as in step 1; then cut 2 border strips, 42½" long (or the width of your quilt top) from the long strip. Sew these to the top and bottom of the quilt.

3. To make the middle border, piece together 3 of the 1½" muslin strips. From this long strip, cut 2 strips 58½" long (or the length of your quilt top). Sew them to the long sides of your quilt top. Piece together 3 more strips and cut 2 strips 44½" long or the width of your quilt. Sew them to the top and bottom of the quilt.

4. You'll need 104 blue flying-geese units for the middle border. These are made in the same manner as the star points on page 107. To make a flying-geese unit, place a 2½" muslin square on top of a 2½" x 4½" blue rectangle, right sides together, raw edges even. Sew across the diagonal.

5. Cut off the outer corner, leaving a ¼" seam allowance, and press back the remaining triangle. Repeat on the opposite side to complete a flying-geese unit. Repeat to make 104 units.

Make 104.

6. To make a Square-in-a-Square border corner block, place a 2½" muslin square on top of a 4½" blue square, right sides together, corner edges even. Sew across the diagonal as shown, just as you did for the flying-geese units.

7. Cut off the outer corner, leaving a ¼" seam allowance, and press back the remaining triangle. Repeat on all corners to complete 1 corner block. Make a total of 4.

Make 4.

8. Sew 30 blue flying-geese units together, end to end. Repeat to make 2 long borders. Sew them to the long sides of the quilt. The "geese" should be pointing upward on the left border and downward on the right border.

9. Sew 22 flying-geese units together. Repeat to make 2 borders. Add a corner block to both ends of each border. Sew the borders to the top and bottom of the quilt, with the "geese" pointing to the right in the top border and to the left in the bottom border.

10. To complete the middle border, sew 4 of the remaining muslin 1½" strips together in pairs. From the long strips, cut 2 borders, 1½" x 68½". Sew them to the long sides of your quilt. Sew the remaining 3 muslin 1½" strips together, and from this strip cut 2 borders, 1½" x 54½", and sew them to the short sides of the quilt.

11. To make the outer border, sew 4 of the blue 1½" strips together in pairs. From the long strips, cut 2 borders, 1½" x 70½". Sew them to the long sides of the quilt. Sew the remaining 3 blue 1½" strips together, and from this long strip cut 2 borders, 1½" x 56½". Sew them to the top and bottom of the quilt.

Finishing

Refer to "Quilting" on page 11 and "Binding Your Quilt" on page 12 for more detailed instructions on finishing techniques, if needed.

1. Piece the quilt backing so it is 4" larger than the quilt top.

2. Layer the quilt top with batting and backing, and baste the layers together.

3. Quilt and bind using your favorite method.

God bless America

land that I love...

and guide her . . .

Stand beside her

God Bless America
Wall Hanging and Pillow

A perfect duo for a Fourth of July gathering or to display your love of the stars and stripes year-round, this wall hanging and pillow are both quick and easy to assemble. While you have your scrap basket out, you may want to go ahead and stitch another set for a friend.

Finished wall hanging size: 22½" x 22½"
Finished pillow size: 16" x 16"
Finished block size: 8" x 8"

Materials for Wall Hanging and Pillow

Yardage is based on 42"-wide fabric unless otherwise stated.

⅜ yd. tea-dyed muslin for sashing

Scraps of assorted red, white, and gold prints for Flag blocks

Scraps (at least 5" square) of assorted dark blues for Flag blocks and corner squares

1 yd. fabric for backing of wall hanging

¼ yd. dark blue for binding

⅝ yd. red check for border and backing of pillow

26" x 26" piece of batting for wall hanging

18" x 18" piece of batting for pillow

⅛ yd. fusible web (17" wide)

Black embroidery floss

Water-soluble fabric marker for pillow

Permanent black marking pen with ultra-fine point for pillow

5 red buttons

16" x 16" pillow form

Cutting for Wall Hanging

Pattern for the star is on page 114.

From the assorted red scraps, cut:
8 pieces, 1½" x 4½"
8 pieces, 1½" x 8½"

From the assorted light scraps, cut:
8 pieces, 1½" x 4½"
8 pieces, 1½" x 8½"

From the assorted blues, cut:
4 squares, 4½" x 4½"
9 squares, 2½" x 2½"

From the muslin, cut:
12 pieces, 2½" x 8½"

From the assorted gold scraps, cut:
4 stars

From the dark blue yardage, cut:
3 binding strips, 2½" x 42"

Piecing the Flag Blocks for the Wall Hanging

1. Sew two 4½" red strips and two 4½" light strips together, alternating red and light. Repeat to make 4 units.

Make 4.

2. Sew two 8½" red strips and two 8½" light strips together, again alternating red and light. Repeat to make 4 units.

Make 4.

3. Sew a 4½" striped block to a blue square, making sure the blue square is on the left and a red strip is on top. Sew the resulting unit to the

8½" unit from step 2, as shown. Repeat to make 4 Flag blocks.

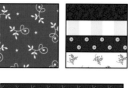

Make 4.

Assembling the Wall Hanging

1. Sew 3 blue 2½" corner squares and 2 muslin 8½" sashing strips together, as shown. Repeat to create 3 rows.

Make 3.

2. Join the blocks and muslin sashing strips side by side, as shown. Alternating sashing rows and block rows, sew the quilt together as shown.

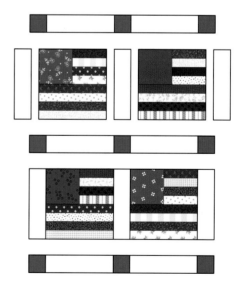

3. Referring to "Using Fusible Web" on page 8, prepare the gold stars for appliqué. Fuse the stars on the blue squares of the Flag blocks. Then stitch around the star edges using a blanket stitch with 2 strands of black embroidery floss.

Finishing the Wall Hanging

Refer to "Quilting" on page 11 and "Binding Your Quilt" on page 12 for more detailed instructions on finishing techniques, if needed.

1. Trim the backing so it is 4" larger than the quilt top.
2. Layer the quilt top with batting and backing, and baste the layers together.
3. Quilt and bind using your favorite method.

Cutting for the Pillow

Pattern for the star is below right.

From the assorted red scraps, cut:
2 pieces, 1½" x 4½"
2 pieces, 1½" x 8½"

From the assorted light scraps, cut:
2 pieces, 1½" x 4½"
2 pieces, 1½" x 8½"

From the assorted blue scraps, cut:
1 square, 4½" x 4½"
4 squares, 2½" x 2½"

From the muslin, cut:
4 pieces, 2½" x 8½"

From the gold scrap, cut:
1 star

From the red check, cut:
2 strips, 2½" x 12½"
2 strips, 2½" x 16½"
1 square, 16½" x 16½"

Making the Pillow Top

1. Referring to "Piecing the Flag Blocks for the Wall Hanging" on page 113, make 1 Flag block.
2. Referring to step 3 of "Assembling the Wall Hanging" on page 113, appliqué a gold star in place. Stitch around the appliqué with 2 strands of black embroidery floss.

3. Sew a 2½" x 12½" red check border strip to the top and bottom of the Flag block. Sew a 2½" x 16½" red check border strip to the sides of the Flag block.
4. Using the water-soluble fabric marker, write the following words on the muslin sashing strips.
   Top: God bless America
   Right: land that I love.
   Bottom: Stand beside her
   Left: and guide her . . .
5. When you are satisfied with your lettering placement, trace over the words with the permanent black marking pen.

Finishing the Pillow

Quilting the pillow top is optional. Place the pillow top and pillow back (16½" square of red check fabric) right sides together. Pin the edges, then sew around the edges using a ¼" seam allowance. Leave a 12" opening along one edge. Clip the corners, turn the pillow covering right side out, and press, turning under ¼" along the unsewn edges. Stuff with the 16" pillow form and slipstitch the opening shut.

Star

Grand Old Flag

Finished quilt size: 40½" x 40½"
Finished block size: 20" x 20"

Display your patriotism and love of Americana with this simple wall hanging. I designed this project for my own family room, where it currently hangs. If you'd like your quilt to have a bit more of a rustic touch, consider a plaid or check border. You could even make each side of the border out of a different fabric.

Materials

Yardage is based on 42"-wide fabric unless otherwise stated.

1½ yds. blue toile for border

¼ yd. *each* of 4 different red prints for flag stripes

¼ yd. *each* of 4 different ivory prints for flag stripes

16 different scraps of blue for stars

16 different scraps of ivory for star backgrounds

2½ yds. fabric for backing

½ yd. fabric for binding

44" x 44" piece of batting

½ yd. fusible web (17" wide)

Cutting

Pattern for the star is on page 117.

From *each* of the 16 blue scraps, cut:
1 star

From *each* of the 16 ivory scraps, cut:
1 square, 3" x 3"

From the red prints, cut:
2 strips, 3" x 10½"
2 strips, 3" x 20½"

From the ivory prints, cut:
2 strips, 3" x 10½"
2 strips, 3" x 20½"

From the blue toile, cut:★
2 strips, 10½" x 20½", for side borders
2 strips, 10½" x 40½", for top and bottom borders

From the binding fabric, cut:
5 strips, 2½" x 42"

★ *If your print is directional like mine, cut the top and bottom border strips across the width of the fabric. Then cut the side borders along the length (parallel to selvages).*

Making the Flag Block

1. Referring to "Using Fusible Web" on page 8, prepare the stars for appliqué.

2. Fuse a star onto each of the 16 ivory squares, placing them so that some of the stars are randomly tilted, as shown. (Be sure the stars don't extend into the seam allowance.) When you're satisfied with their placement, stitch around the star edges using blue or black thread and a machine blanket stitch.

3. Sew the star squares together in rows, then sew the rows together.

4. Sew the 10½" red and ivory strips together, alternating colors.

5. Join the unit made in step 4 to the completed star unit. Be sure to place a red strip at the top of the flag.

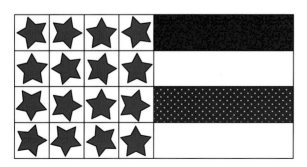

6. Sew the 20½" red and ivory strips together, alternating colors. Sew this unit to the one made in step 5, with a red strip adjoining the bottom of the star unit.

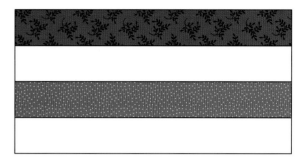

Adding the Border

Sew the 10½" x 20½" blue toile border strips to the sides of the Flag block. Then add the 10½" x 40½" border strips to the top and bottom.

Finishing

Refer to "Quilting" on page 11 and "Binding Your Quilt" on page 12 for more detailed instructions on finishing techniques, if needed.

1. Piece the quilt backing so it is 4" larger than the quilt top.

2. Layer the quilt top with batting and backing, and baste the layers together.

3. Quilt and bind using your favorite method.

Star

Paddleboat

Finished quilt size: 48" x 48"
Finished block size: 14" x 14"

Materials

Yardage is based on 42"-wide fabric.

2 yds. ivory print for blocks and border

1½ yds. red gingham for border

⅞ yd. red print for blocks and binding

½ yd. blue gingham for blocks

⅜ yd. light blue print for triangle border

3¼ yds. fabric for backing

53" x 53" piece of batting

Cutting

From the ivory print, cut:
2 strips, 4½" x 32½"
2 strips, 4½" x 40½"
12 squares, 2⅞" x 2⅞"
19 strips, 2½" x 42"; from these strips, cut:
    144 squares, 2½" x 2½"
    28 rectangles, 2½" x 4½"
    16 rectangles, 2½" x 6½"

From the red print, cut:
4 squares, 2½" x 2½"
16 rectangles, 2½" x 4½"
8 squares, 2⅞" x 2⅞"
6 binding strips, 2½" x 42"

From the light blue, cut:
2 squares, 2⅞" x 2⅞"
4 strips, 2½" x 42"; crosscut into 56 squares, 2½" x 2½"

From the red gingham, cut lengthwise:
2 strips, 2½" x 44½"
2 strips, 2½" x 48½"
40 rectangles, 2½" x 4½"
2 squares, 2⅞" x 2⅞"

From the blue gingham, cut:
5 strips, 2½" x 42"; from these strips, cut:
    16 rectangles, 2½" x 6½"
    16 rectangles, 2½" x 4½"

My Paddleboat block is a variation of a traditional block that goes by many different names, of which "Duck Paddle" is one of the more descriptive. Pieced in a fresh red, white, and light blue color scheme, this block reminded me of sunny summer days spent at the seaside—thus the name Paddleboat! Whatever you choose to call it, this four-block quilt is made with time-saving piecing techniques, so it's quick and easy.

Piecing the Blocks

1. With a pencil, draw a line across the diagonal on the wrong side of all twelve 2⅞" ivory squares.

2. Place a 2⅞" red print square and a 2⅞" ivory square right sides together. Sew ¼" from the marked line on both sides of the line. Cut apart on the line; press the 2 triangle squares open. Using the remaining 2⅞" red print squares and 7 of the ivory 2⅞" squares, repeat to make a total of 16 triangle squares.

119

3. Using 2 light blue 2⅞" squares and 2 ivory 2⅞" squares, repeat step 2 to make 4 triangle squares. Set these aside for the inner border.

4. Using the remaining 2 ivory 2⅞" squares and the red gingham 2⅞" squares, repeat step 2 to make 4 triangle squares. Set these aside for the outer border.

5. Sew the red-print-and-ivory triangle squares to 2½" ivory squares, as shown. (Be careful not to use the red gingham triangle squares.) You need 16 units.

6. Place a 2½" ivory square on top of a red print 2½" x 4½" rectangle, right sides together, and sew across the diagonal of the ivory square, as shown. Cut off the outer corner, leaving a ¼" seam allowance, and press the remaining ivory triangle back. Repeat to make 16 of these units.

Make 16.

7. Using the 2½" x 4½" blue gingham rectangles and 2½" ivory squares, follow the same procedures as in step 6, except sew across the opposite corner, as shown. Repeat to make 16 of these units.

Make 16.

8. Using the 2½" x 6½" blue gingham rectangles and 2½" ivory squares, again follow the procedure in step 6. This time, stitch across the same corner as in the red and ivory units. Repeat to make 16 units.

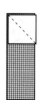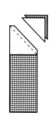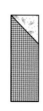

Make 16.

9. Piece together 16 paddle units, as shown.

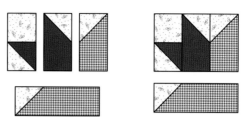

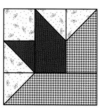

Make 16.

10. Sew a paddle unit to either side of an ivory 2½" x 6½" rectangle, as shown. Repeat to make 8 of these units.

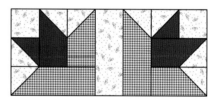

Make 8.

11. Sew a 2½" x 6½" ivory rectangle to either side of a 2½" red print square. Make 4 of these units.

Make 4.

12. Piece the units together to make 4 Paddleboat blocks, as shown.

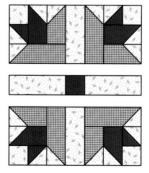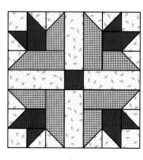

Make 4.

Assembling the Quilt Top

Sew together the 4 blocks in 2 rows of 2 blocks. Join the rows to create the center of the quilt.

Adding the Border

1. The border includes flying-geese units in 2 color combinations. Start with the light-blue-and-ivory flying-geese units. You'll need 28, 7 for each side of the quilt. To make each unit, place a 2½" light blue square on top of a 2½" x 4½" ivory rectangle, right sides together. Sew across the diagonal. Cut off the outer corner, leaving a ¼" seam allowance, and press the remaining triangle back. Repeat on the other side.

Make 28.

2. Sew 7 flying-geese units together, end to end. Repeat to make 4 identical borders.

Make 4.

3. Sew a flying-geese border to the right and left sides of the quilt, making sure the light blue fabric adjoins the quilt center on all sides.

4. Using the light-blue-and-ivory triangle squares from step 3 of "Piecing the Blocks" on page 120, sew 1 triangle square to each end of the remaining 2 flying-geese borders, as shown. (Make sure your triangle squares face the right direction.) Then sew the borders to the top and bottom of the quilt.

Make 2.

5. Sew the 4½" x 32½" ivory border strips to the right and left sides of the quilt. Then sew the 4½" x 40½" ivory border strips to the top and bottom of the quilt.

6. Using the method described in step 1 at left, create 40 flying-geese units using 2½" x 4½" red gingham rectangles and 2½" ivory squares.

Make 40.

7. Sew 10 red gingham flying-geese units together, end to end. Repeat to create 4 borders of 10 units each.

Make 4.

8. Sew a flying-geese border to the right and left sides of the quilt, making sure the ivory triangles adjoin the ivory borders.

9. Sew the 4 red-gingham-and-ivory triangle squares from step 4 of "Piecing the Blocks" on page 120 to the ends of the remaining 2 flying-geese borders, as shown. (Make sure your triangle squares face the right direction.) Then sew the borders to the top and bottom of the quilt.

Make 4.

10. Sew the 2½" x 44½" red gingham border strips to the sides of the quilt and the 2½" x 48½" red gingham border strips to the top and bottom of the quilt.

Finishing

Refer to "Quilting" on page 11 and "Binding Your Quilt" on page 12 for more detailed instructions on finishing techniques, if needed.

1. Piece the quilt backing so it is 4" larger than the quilt top.
2. Layer the quilt top with batting and backing, and baste the layers together.
3. Quilt and bind using your favorite method.

Autumn Ridge

Finished quilt size: 60½" x 75½"
Finished block size: 7½" x 7½"

Materials

Yardage is based on 42"-wide fabric unless otherwise stated.

⅛ yd. *each* or scraps of assorted golds, yellows, and tans to total 2¼ yds.

⅛ yd. *each* or scraps of assorted purples to total 1¼ yds.

⅛ yd. *each* or scraps of assorted dark reds and oranges to total 1¼ yds.

⅛ yd. *each* or scraps of assorted dark greens to total 1¼ yds.

4½ yds. fabric for backing

⅝ yd. fabric for binding

65" x 80" piece of batting

Cutting

From the assorted golds, yellows, and tans, cut:
64 squares, 2" x 2"
64 rectangles, 2" x 3½"
64 rectangles, 2" x 5"
64 strips, 2" x 6½"
32 strips, 2" x 8"

From *each* color group of purples, reds, and greens, cut:
32 squares, 2" x 2" (96 total)
32 rectangles, 2" x 3½" (96 total)
32 rectangles, 2" x 5" (96 total)
32 strips, 2" x 6½" (96 total)
16 strips, 2" x 8" (48 total)

From the binding fabric, cut:
7 strips, 2½" x 42"

The quantities given above are the exact amounts needed, but I suggest that you don't cut all the Log Cabin pieces at once. Cut enough to get started, then adjust colors and prints as you go, cutting additional pieces when you need them. Keep the strips organized by color and length.

This stunning quilt is easy to make with simple Log Cabin blocks. At first, I made my blocks with too many bright reds and greens: it came out looking Christmassy. Then I remade the quilt, using deeper wine reds and yellow-based greens to achieve the autumn feeling. I even threw in some orange fabrics. Be sure to include prints of large, medium, and small scale.

Piecing the Log Cabin Blocks

When you assemble the blocks for the quilt, the dominant (determining) color of each block will be the color of the 8" strip, so pay attention to the "top" color; the blocks cannot be rotated.

1. Start by making 16 blocks with reds on top and golds on the bottom. Sew a red 2" square and a gold 2" square together. Press the seam allowance toward the darker fabric.

2. Add a 3½" gold strip. Press the seam allowance (and all future seam allowances) toward the newest strip.

3. Working your way around the block in a counterclockwise direction, add a 3½" red strip followed by a 5" red strip.

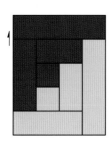

4. Add a 5" gold strip, followed by a 6½" gold strip.

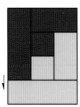

5. Add a 6½" red strip, followed by an 8" red strip to complete the block.

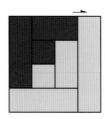

6. Repeat steps 1–5 to make a total of 16 blocks with 5 red strips and 4 gold strips.

7. Now repeat steps 1–5 to piece 16 blocks with gold on top (5 gold strips) and red on the bottom (4 red strips).

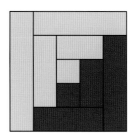

Make 16.

8. Repeat steps 1–5 to make Log Cabin blocks in the following color combinations. You should have a total of 80 Log Cabin blocks.

Number Needed	Color Combination
8	Gold on top and green on bottom
8	Green on top and purple on bottom
8	Purple on top and gold on bottom
8	Gold on top and purple on bottom
8	Purple on top and green on bottom
8	Green on top and gold on bottom

Arranging and Sewing the Rows

1. Lay out 10 rows of 8 blocks each, referring to the assembly diagram and the following list. Remember that every block has a dominant color (the top color, with 5 strips rather than 4). Do not rotate the blocks.

   Row 1: Red on top, gold on bottom
   Row 2: Gold on top, green on bottom
   Row 3: Green on top, purple on bottom
   Row 4: Purple on top, gold on bottom
   Row 5: Gold on top, red on bottom
   Row 6: Red on top, gold on bottom
   Row 7: Gold on top, purple on bottom

Row 8: Purple on top, green on bottom
Row 9: Green on top, gold on bottom
Row 10: Gold on top, red on bottom

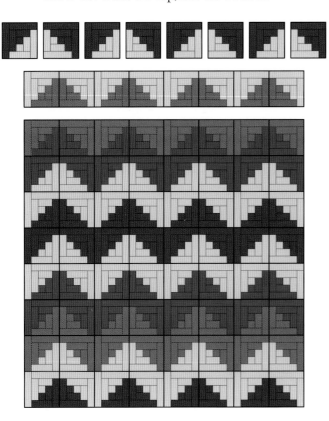

2. You'll see a zigzag pattern emerge as you add rows of blocks. Maintaining the correct color placement, move individual Log Cabin blocks until the brights, darks, and busiest prints are nicely balanced across the quilt.

Fine-Tuning Your Fabrics

Scrap quilts have a tendency to take on a life of their own. If at this point your quilt doesn't look quite the way you want it to—maybe it's too dark or too bland—then by all means, make changes now. Sometimes just replacing a few of the 8" strips will do the trick. Or you may have to discard entire blocks and remake them. Simply remaking a handful of blocks can alter an entire quilt: much better to do it now than regret it after the quilt is finished.

3. Sew the blocks together in rows, stitching 8 blocks across, side by side.
4. Sew the 10 rows together, working from top to bottom.

Finishing

Refer to "Quilting" on page 11 and "Binding Your Quilt" on page 12 for more detailed instructions on finishing techniques, if needed.

1. Piece the quilt backing so it is 4" larger than the quilt top.
2. Layer the quilt top with batting and backing, and baste the layers together.
3. Quilt and bind using your favorite method.

Cottage Plaid

Finished quilt size: 43¼" x 52½"
Finished block size: 6½" x 6½"

Materials

Yardage is based on 42"-wide fabric.

2¼ yds. light print for blocks, setting triangles, corner triangles, and border

⅞ yd. dark print for patchwork and binding

¾ yd. medium print for patchwork

2¾ yds. fabric for backing

48" x 57" piece of batting

Cutting

From the light print, cut:
15 strips, 2" x 42"; crosscut 8 of these strips into
   80 pieces, 2" x 3½"
4 squares, 11½" x 11½"
2 squares, 6" x 6"
5 strips, 3½" x 42"

From the dark print, cut:
6 strips, 1" x 42"; crosscut into 64 pieces, 1" x 3½"
7 strips, 1" x 42"; crosscut into 32 rectangles, 1" x 7"
5 strips, 2½" x 42"

From the medium print, cut:
12 strips, 2" x 42"; crosscut 5 of these strips into
   48 pieces, 2" x 3½"

One thing that makes this quilt interesting is the combination of a masculine, graphic pattern with a feminine toile print. I used green toile for the light color, a green check for the medium, and an "almost solid" for the dark. This quilt is perfect for a family room throw—or alter the color scheme for an intriguing baby quilt.

Piecing the Blocks

Review the directions in "Assembly-Line Machine Piecing" on pages 7–8. You will need to make 20 light blocks and 12 medium blocks to complete this quilt.

1. Sew a 2" x 42" light strip to a 2" x 42" medium strip lengthwise. Repeat to make 7 of these strip sets.

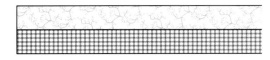

Make 7 strip sets.

2. Cut the strip sets into 2" sections. You need 128 of these segments.

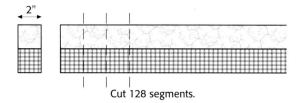

Cut 128 segments.

3. Join 2 of the segments made in step 2 to either side of a 1" x 3½" dark strip. Repeat to make a total of 64 units.

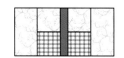

Make 64.

4. Add a 2" x 3½" light rectangle to both sides of 40 of the units made in step 3. Reserve the remaining 24 units.

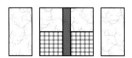

Make 40.

5. Join 2 units from step 4 and a 1" x 7" dark strip as shown to complete a light block. Make a total of 20 light blocks.

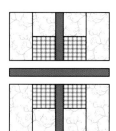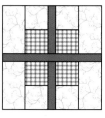

Make 20.

6. Add a 2" x 3½" medium rectangle to both sides of the remaining units made in step 3.

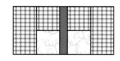

Make 24.

7. Join 2 of the units made in step 6 to a 1" x 7" dark strip to complete a medium block. Repeat to make a total of 12 medium blocks.

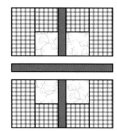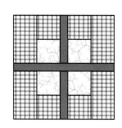

Make 12.

Assembling the Quilt Top

1. To make side setting triangles, cut the four 11½" light squares in half diagonally in both directions. Make the corner triangles by cutting the 6" light squares across one diagonal only.

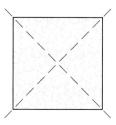

2. Alternating light and medium blocks, assemble the blocks and triangles in diagonal rows, as shown in the diagram on the following page. Sew on the corner triangles last. To achieve the

plaid illusion, make sure the dark center strips line up properly throughout.

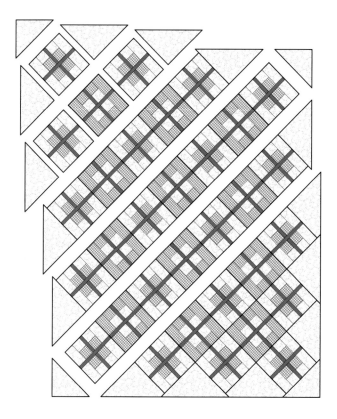

3. Trim the excess triangle fabric, leaving a ¼" seam allowance all the way around the quilt.

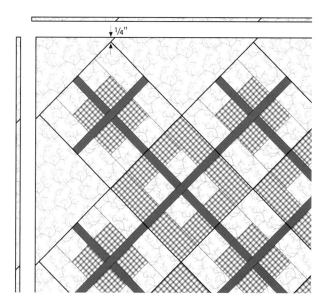

Trim edges, leaving a ¼" seam allowance.

Adding the Border

1. Measure the length of the quilt through the center. Sew 3 of the light 3½" strips together end to end. From this long strip, cut 2 strips the length of your quilt. Sew the border strips to the long sides of your quilt.
2. Measure the width of the quilt through the center, including the side borders you just added. Cut the remaining 2 light 3½" strips to this length. Sew the border strips to the top and bottom of the quilt.

Finishing

Refer to "Quilting" on page 11 and "Binding Your Quilt" on page 12 for more detailed instructions on finishing techniques, if needed.

1. Piece the quilt backing so it is 4" larger than the quilt top.
2. Layer the quilt top with batting and backing, and baste the layers together.
3. Quilt and bind using your favorite method.

Twenty-Five Patch

Finished quilt size: 62½" x 86½"
Finished block size: 10" x 10"

Materials

Yardage is based on 42"-wide fabric.

⅛ yd. *each* of 35 assorted light prints for blocks

⅛ yd. *each* of 35 medium-dark prints for blocks

2¼ yds. beige print for sashing and border

¼ yd. green for corner squares

5½ yds. fabric for backing

¾ yd. fabric for binding

67" x 91" piece of batting

Cutting

From *each* of the 35 light prints, cut:
2 rectangles, 2½" x 8"
3 rectangles, 2½" x 5½"

From *each* of the 35 medium-dark prints, cut:
3 rectangles, 2½" x 8"
2 rectangles, 2½" x 5½"

From the beige print, cut:
28 strips, 2½" x 42"; crosscut into 82 pieces,
    2½" x 10½"

From the green, cut:
48 squares, 2½" x 2½"

From the binding fabric, cut:
8 strips, 2½" x 42"

There are 35 patchwork blocks in this quilt, each made from only two fabrics—one light and one medium-dark pastel. Choosing the fabrics for this one is a lot of fun, and it's a great way to mix and match scraps that you have on hand.

Piecing the Blocks

1. Review the directions in "Assembly-Line Piecing" on pages 7–8. For each patchwork block, you need 2 light 8" rectangles, 3 light 5½" rectangles, 3 medium-dark 8" rectangles, and 2 medium-dark 5½" rectangles.

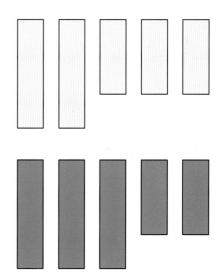

2. Alternating colors, sew the 8" rectangles together. In the same manner, sew the 5½" rectangles together. Press all seam allowances in one direction.

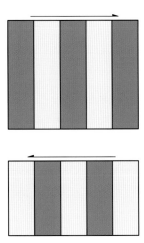

3. Cut the units into 2½" segments. You need 5 segments for each block—3 with darker squares on the outside and 2 with lighter squares on the outside. Discard any leftovers.

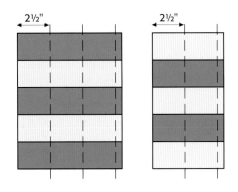

4. Sew the segments together as shown to complete a Twenty-Five Patch block. Press seam allowances in alternate directions to reduce bulk.

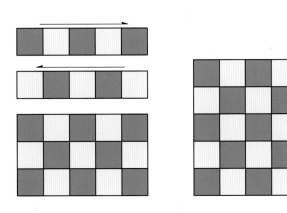

5. Repeat steps 1–4 to make 35 Twenty-Five Patch blocks.

Assembling the Quilt Top

1. Lay out all the blocks on a design wall or floor, arranging them in rows 5 across and 7 deep. Take the time to find the most appealing arrangement of colors and prints.

2. When you are pleased with the quilt layout, sew together a row of 5 blocks alternating with 6 beige sashing strips, as shown. Repeat for all 7 horizontal rows.

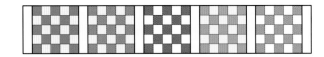

3. To make the sashing rows, alternate 6 green 2½" corner squares with 5 beige sashing strips, and sew the pieces together. Repeat to make 8 sashing rows.

4. Sew the block and sashing rows together to complete the quilt top.

Finishing

Refer to "Quilting" on page 11 and "Binding Your Quilt" on page 12 for more detailed instructions on finishing techniques, if needed.

1. Piece the quilt backing so it is 4" larger than the quilt top.

2. Layer the quilt top with batting and backing, and baste the layers together.

3. Quilt and bind using your favorite method.

Duck and Ducklings

Subtle shades of pink and green add old-fashioned charm to a traditional quilt block pattern. The Dogtooth border is one of my favorites, softening the edges and giving the illusion of a scalloped border.

Finished quilt size: 51½" x 51½"
Finished block size: 9" x 9"

Materials

Yardage is based on 42"-wide fabric.

1½ yds. light print for block background and sashing

1⅜ yds. pink floral print for outer border

1 yd. green for blocks and binding

¼ yd. medium pink for blocks

⅛ yd. pale pink for sashing squares

3¼ yds. fabric for backing

56" x 56" piece of batting

Cutting

From the light print, cut:

4 strips, 2" x 42"; crosscut into 36 rectangles, 2" x 4¼"

4 strips, 2¾" x 42"; crosscut into 54 squares, 2¾" x 2¾"; cut once diagonally to yield 108 triangles

3 strips, 3½" x 42"; crosscut into 12 pieces, 3½" x 9½"

2 strips, 2" x 33½"

2 strips, 2" x 36½"

5 strips, 2" x 42"; crosscut into 96 squares, 2" x 2"

2 squares, 2⅜" x 2⅜"

From the medium pink, cut:

9 squares, 2" x 2"

18 squares, 2¾" x 2¾"; cut once diagonally to yield 36 triangles

From the green, cut:

18 squares, 4⅝" x 4⅝"; cut once diagonally to yield 36 triangles

6 strips, 2½" x 42"

From the pink floral print, cut:

5 strips, 2" x 42"; crosscut into 48 pieces, 2" x 3½"

2 squares, 2⅜" x 2⅜"

2 strips, 6½" x 39½"

2 strips, 6½" x 51½"

From the pale pink, cut:

4 squares, 3½" x 3½"

Piecing the Blocks

Refer to the instructions in "Assembly-Line Machine Piecing" on pages 7–8 as needed.

1. Assemble the following for 1 Duck and Ducklings block: 12 triangles and 4 rectangles cut from the light print, 4 triangles and 1 square cut from the medium pink, and 4 triangles cut from the green.

2. Sew each of the four 2¾" medium pink triangles to 2¾" light triangles, as shown.

Make 4.

3. Sew a light triangle to the sides of the triangle squares made in step 2, as shown. Sew the pieced triangles to the 4⅝" green triangles to make 4 pieced units.

Make 4.

4. Join the medium pink square to 2 light rectangles to make a center strip.
5. Piece the units together as shown to complete 1 block. Repeat to make a total of 9 Duck and Ducklings blocks.

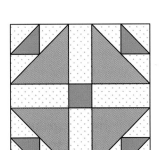

Make 9.

Assembling the Quilt Top

1. Join 3 completed Duck and Ducklings blocks together, using two 3½" x 9½" light print sashing strips, as shown. Make 3 such rows.

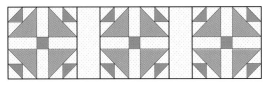

Make 3.

2. Sew 2 pale pink squares and 3 light 3½" x 9½" sashing strips together, as shown. Make 2 of these units.

Make 2.

3. Alternating block and sashing rows, sew the rows together.

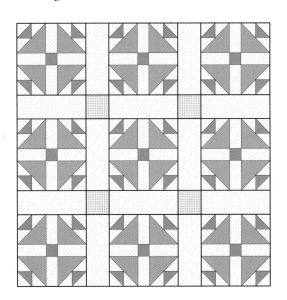

Adding the Border

1. Sew the 2" x 33½" light print border strips to the sides of the quilt. Sew the 2" x 36½" border strips to the top and bottom of the quilt.

2. To make the pink-and-white dogtooth border, start by making 48 flying-geese units. To make a flying-geese unit, place a 2" light square on top of a 2" x 3½" pink floral rectangle, with right sides together and edges even.

3. Stitch across the diagonal. Cut off the outer corner, leaving a ¼" seam allowance, and press back the remaining triangle.

4. Repeat steps 2 and 3 on the opposite end of the rectangle to complete a flying-geese unit. Repeat to make a total of 48 units.

Make 48.

5. For the border corners, use a pencil to draw a diagonal line across both 2⅜" light squares on the wrong side of the fabric. Place each marked square on top of a pink floral 2⅜" square, right sides together. Sew ¼" away from the guideline, on both sides of the line as shown.

6. Cut the squares apart on the pencil guideline. Press open to create a total of 4 corner triangle squares.

7. Sew 12 flying-geese units together side by side to make a dogtooth border. Repeat to create 4 such borders.

Make 4.

8. Sew a dogtooth border to the left and right sides of the quilt, making sure that the light print side of the border adjoins the quilt center.

9. Sew the corner triangle squares made in step 6 to each end of the top and bottom flying-geese borders. Make sure the corners are rotated properly to continue the zigzag pattern. Then sew the borders to the top and bottom of the quilt.

Make 2.

10. Sew the 6½" x 39½" pink floral border strips to the left and right sides of the quilt. Sew the 6½" x 51½" border strips to the top and bottom of the quilt.

Finishing

Refer to "Quilting" on page 11 and "Binding Your Quilt" on page 12 for more detailed instructions on finishing techniques, if needed.

1. Piece the quilt backing so it is 4" larger than the quilt top.

2. Layer the quilt top with batting and backing, and baste the layers together.

3. Quilt and bind using your favorite method.

Sand Castles

One day I looked at my fabric stash and realized I had a lot of vintage-style floral pieces that were too small for anything but a scrap quilt. This project was the result, and it was an indulgent joy to create. I got to play with a lot of pretty fabrics and the blocks were a breeze to sew.

Finished quilt size: 65½" x 76½"
Finished block size: 7½" x 7½"

Materials

Yardage is based on 42"-wide fabric.

2 yds. pink floral print for border

¼ yd. *each* of at least 15 different floral prints (use even more for a truly scrappy look)

1 yd. muslin for blocks

4½ yds. fabric for backing

¾ yd. fabric for binding

70" x 81" piece of batting

Cutting

From the floral prints, cut:
72 squares, 8" x 8"; cut each square in half in both directions (not diagonally) to make 4 matching squares, 4" x 4" (288 squares total)

From the muslin, cut:
15 strips, 1" x 42"; crosscut into 144 pieces, 1" x 4"
15 strips, 1" x 42"; crosscut into 72 pieces, 1" x 8"

From the pink floral print, cut lengthwise:
2 strips, 6½" x 64"
2 strips, 6½" x 65"

From the binding fabric, cut:
8 strips, 2½" x 42"

Piecing the Blocks

For each block, you will use 4 matching floral squares, two 4" muslin strips, and one 8" muslin strip.

1. Sew a floral square to either side of a 4" muslin strip. Repeat to make 2 units.

2. Piece the 2 units to either side of an 8" muslin strip to complete 1 block. Repeat to make a total of 72 blocks.

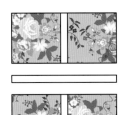

Make 72.

Assembling the Quilt Top

1. Lay out the completed blocks in diagonal rows until you find the most pleasing arrangement. There are 6 "points" across the top and bottom and 7 "points" down each side. When you're satisfied with the arrangement, sew the blocks together in diagonal rows. Then join the rows, being careful to align the center muslin stripes to create the overall crisscross pattern.

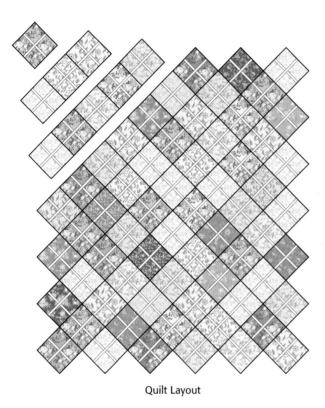

Quilt Layout

2. Using a rotary cutter and a ruler, trim off the outer block "points" to square up the quilt. Be sure to leave a ¼" seam allowance past the

points of the inner blocks, as shown. Take care to keep the quilt's corners perfectly square.

Trim ¼" away from inner points of blocks.

Adding the Border

1. Measure the length of the quilt through the center. It should measure approximately 64". (If not, see "Adding Borders" on page 10.) Then sew the 6½" x 64" (or length of your quilt) pink floral border strips to both sides.
2. Measure the width of the quilt through the center, including the side borders. It should measure approximately 65". Sew the 6½" x 65" (or width of your quilt) border strips to the top and bottom of the quilt.

Finishing

Refer to "Quilting" on page 11 and "Binding Your Quilt" on page 12 for more detailed instructions on finishing techniques, if needed.

1. Piece the quilt backing so it is 4" larger than the quilt top.
2. Layer the quilt top with batting and backing, and baste the layers together.
3. Quilt and bind using your favorite method.

Grandma's Dishes

Finished quilt size: 64½" x 72½"
Finished block size: 8" x 8"

Materials

Yardage is based on 42"-wide fabric.

8 to 15 different medium-colored prints for blocks
(1¾ yds. total)

8 to 15 different light-colored prints for blocks
(1¾ yds. total)

2 yds. white print for inner border

2 yds. aqua check for outer border

4½ yds. fabric for backing

¾ yd. fabric for binding

69" x 77" batting

4½ yds. fusible web (17" wide)

Cutting

The pattern for the quarter-circle is on page 143.

From the medium-colored prints, cut:
15 squares, 8½" x 8½"
108 quarter-circles

From the light-colored prints, cut:
15 squares, 8½" x 8½"
60 quarter-circles

From the white print, cut:
26 squares, 8½" x 8½"

From the aqua check, cut on the length of grain:
4 strips, 4½" x 64½"

From the binding fabric, cut:
8 strips, 2½" x 42"

The circular shapes as well as the colors in this quilt call to mind the vintage dishes that are so popular today. Appliqué, not curved piecing, creates the circles. Be sure to choose distinctive groupings of light- and medium-colored fabrics for your circles: I used pastels for a subtle effect, but if you choose stronger colors the circle design will be more prominent.

Making the Appliqué Blocks

1. Referring to "Using Fusible Web" on page 8, prepare 168 quarter-circles for appliqué. I recommend cutting out the center of each fusible web piece to reduce stiffness in your finished quilt. You need 4 quarter-circles per block for the 30 blocks, and 48 for the inner border.

2. Fuse 108 of the quarter-circles onto the wrong side of many different medium-colored prints. Fuse the remaining 60 quarter-circles onto the wrong side of many different light-colored prints. Cut out all 168 shapes on the marked lines. Set aside 48 medium-colored quarter-circles for the inner border.

3. Remove the paper backing from 60 medium-colored quarter-circles. Fuse 4 of them onto each light 8½" square to make 15 blocks.

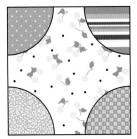

Make 15.

4. Remove the paper backing from 60 light-colored quarter-circles. Fuse 4 of them onto each medium-colored 8½" square to make 15 blocks.

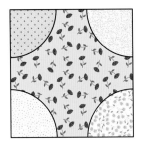

Make 15.

5. Stitch around the curved edge of each quarter-circle using a machine blanket stitch and light-colored thread to blend. The straight outer edges do not need to be sewn since they will be caught in the seams.

Assembling the Quilt Top

1. Lay out all the blocks on a design wall or floor, 5 across and 6 down. Alternating light and medium blocks, move them around until the colors are balanced. (You don't want all the blues in one corner, for example.) Sew the blocks together in rows. Press all seam allowances open to reduce bulk. Then sew the rows together.

2. Assemble the 8½" white print squares and the 48 medium-colored quarter-circles prepared with fusible web. Press 2 quarter-circles onto 22 squares, as shown, to make the side border blocks. Press 1 quarter-circle onto the remaining 4 blocks to make 4 corner border blocks. Stitch around the curved edges only, using a blanket stitch, to complete the 26 blocks.

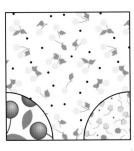
Border Block
Make 22.

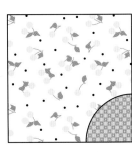
Corner Block
Make 4.

3. Position the border blocks around the quilt center, 6 on each side and 5 across the top and bottom. Move the blocks around until the colors are balanced, then add the appliquéd corner blocks to the top and bottom borders, as shown.

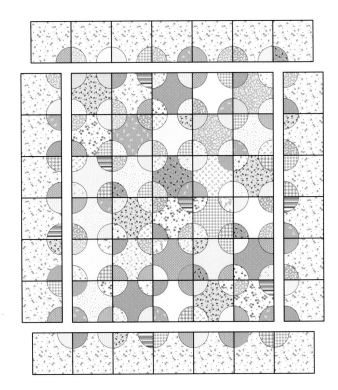

142

4. Sew the side borders first by stitching the 6 side blocks together. Repeat for the opposite side. Sew these to the long sides of the quilt, with the circles next to the quilt center.

5. Sew the top and bottom borders together, with 5 side blocks and a corner block at each end. Sew to the top and bottom of the quilt.

6. Sew two 4½" x 64½" aqua check border strips to the long sides of the quilt. Then sew the remaining 4½" x 64½" border strips to the top and bottom of the quilt.

Finishing

Refer to "Quilting" on page 11 and "Binding Your Quilt" on page 12 for more detailed instructions on finishing techniques, if needed.

1. Piece the quilt backing so it is 4" larger than the quilt top.

2. Layer the quilt top with batting and backing, and baste the layers together.

3. Quilt and bind using your favorite method.

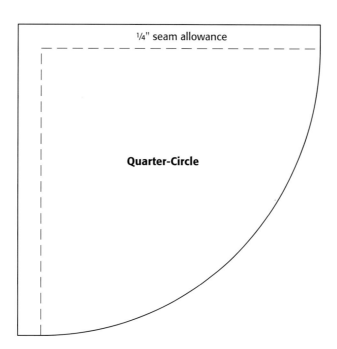

¼" seam allowance

Quarter-Circle

About the Author

Teri Christopherson loves quilting because it allows her to play with color—*and* to buy all the fabric she wants! Her passion was born when her mother taught her, at age five, to use the sewing machine. By the time she was a teenager, Teri was spending all her spare change at the fabric store and sewing all her own clothes.

Teri taught herself to quilt during her college years. She spent more time cutting out squares than studying for midterms—which actually served her well: later, as a young mother in search of a home business, she began selling her quilts in country stores. Business was so good that soon she and her sister, Barbara Brandeburg of Cabbage Rose, were quilting night and day to keep up with the demand.

Her talent and enthusiasm for designing new quilts led Teri to publish her original designs. In 1993, Black Mountain Quilts was formed, named after a mountain near her home in southern California. Teri peddled her first four patterns to local quilt stores but soon rented a booth at the wholesale trade show Quilt Market, where she sold her patterns to stores across the country and the world. Within a year, she had published twelve patterns and her first book, *Patches & Posies*. Nine years later, she has fourteen books and twenty-seven patterns to her credit, with more continually on the way.

Teri and her husband, Mark, have four young children. Their oldest child, Kelsi, was born with Angelman Syndrome, a severe form of mental retardation. Black Mountain Quilts has allowed Teri to care for her children while running a successful business that fulfills her creative talents. Mark, who hesitated to invest the family savings in those first four patterns, is now very grateful that they did.